The Riddle of the Outlaw Bear

and
Other Faith-Building Stories

The Riddle of the Outlaw Bear

and
Other Faith-Building Stories

by
John H. Leeper

Moody Press
Chicago

© 1984 by
JOHN H. LEEPER

All rights reserved

All Scripture quotations are from the Holy Bible: *New International Version*,
© 1978 by the International Bible Society. Used by permission of
Zondervan Bible Publishers.

Library of Congress Cataloging in Publication Data

Leeper, John H., 1949-
  The riddle of the outlaw bear and other faith-building
stories.

  Summary: A collection of eight fables illustrating
Christian principles.
  1. Fables.   2. Children's stories, American.
[1. Fables.   2. Christian life—Fiction.   3. Short
stories] I. Title.
PZ8.2.L38Ri 1984   [Fic]   83-23759
ISBN 0-8024-7352-0

  1 2 3 4 5 6 7 Printing/B + /Year 89 88 87 86 85 84

Printed in the United States of America

I would like to express my heartfelt gratitude to Lou Zenos and Carmen Raspe, whose constant encouragement and technical assistance were invaluable to me while writing and illustrating this book.

Contents

An Introduction
for Parents

Christian apologetics, or the defense of Christianity against its denunciators, has been viewed by Western believers as a meal suited exclusively to the adult palate. The assumption has been that arguments comparing Christianity to opposing ideologies or defending the existence of God in the face of modern scientific discoveries are too complicated for a child's mind to digest. It is for this reason, I am convinced, that during the lengthy evolution of this book, so many adults have asked me one question more than any other: "Why don't you just write a simple little story illustrating a Bible verse?"

I had three specific reasons for developing these fables

9

in the manner in which they appear. (1) Currently, there are hundreds of excellent books in the aforementioned category available to Christian parents. (2) Sometimes, the simple quotation of a biblical truth or passage of Scripture is insufficient to resolve certain inner human conflicts. And (3) the enemies of Christianity have worked under no delusions concerning the ability of a child to grasp the fundamentals of complex ideas.

The first of these reasons is self-explanatory. A wealth of Christian literature exists for children of all ages. Christian parents should view such material as a vital part of their children's training.

My second statement may to some readers border upon the heretical. Nonetheless, for those of us who spent a number of years wandering in the intellectual desert of agnosticism, one fact is indisputable: once the seed of doubt in the truth of the Scripture takes root in a person's mind, the constant repetition of Bible verses or church liturgy seldom suffices to dislodge it. Until the doubt itself is erased, the words will seem hollow and meaningless. It is towards this goal, the eradication of doubt, that most Christian apologists have historically directed their efforts.

My third reason for writing this book should be evident to any parent who reads an elementary school textbook. The fundamental principles of naturalism and humanism are first preached in rudimentary form at that level. The proponents of humanism, perceiving the need to plant the seeds of religious doubt at the earliest possible age, have developed excellent, persuasive instructional material for children. They have recognized that a seed planted early enough may be cultivated another day.

Yet the flaws in a naturalistic philosophy are glaring and simple. In fact, I thought them to be so simple that if they were reduced to some form of literature as basic as a fable, even a child could understand them. That perception gave birth to the following eight stories.

They deal with fundamental issues. And although I recognize that these few pages can do little more than touch the surface of the deep conflict between Christianity and modern humanistic thought, perhaps they can help lay groundwork for a child's future studies in Christian apologetics.

The Riddle of the Outlaw Bear

Long ago, when not many men lived in America and wild animals roamed everywhere, a giant grizzly bear came down from his den on the wild mountain, looking for food. The other animals called him an "outlaw bear," because he found it easier to take what he wanted from others than to work for his food with long, tiring hunts. His huge brown body was scarred from many fights, and he had won all of them. Nature had given him dangerous weapons. He had huge paws, strong legs, long claws and teeth, and a very quick mind that helped him outwit any enemy as strong as himself.

As the outlaw bear prowled the woods at the foot of the

wild mountain, he came upon a wolf who had just killed a deer. The bear walked slowly toward the wolf and said, "That is a fine catch you made, wolf. Thank you for inviting me to dinner. I am very hungry."

The hair along the wolf's back stood up. He bared his white fangs and growled a warning. "This is my food, not yours, bear! I earned it with a long, hard hunt. You have no right to this deer. It is mine!"

The outlaw bear raised up on his back legs. He was over eight feet tall. His huge size and fierce look made the wolf retreat in fear.

"I am an outlaw bear, wolf," the grizzly growled back. "I take what I want by the strength of my paws and the sharpness of my claws and teeth. And your deer is what I want now."

Well, the wolf knew that he was no match for the bear, so he circled around and around the giant outlaw, howling threats at him. "You had better be careful, bear," he warned. "There are many other wolves in these woods. If I bring them here, together we could kill you."

When the outlaw bear heard that, he sat down and scratched the side of his head with one of his great paws, thinking very hard. Finally, he looked down at the ground and said calmly, "That is true, wolf. Enough of your kind could kill even a strong grizzly like myself. But then, a lot of wolves would die or be crippled for the rest of their lives in such a bloody battle. So I believe that your friends will all think it much safer to catch another deer than to risk a fight with an outlaw bear."

The wolf could not answer that. He knew the bear had spoken the truth. However, the outlaw grizzly looked up

14

at the wolf and grinned. Then, he made an offer.

"I want to be fair with you, wolf, so I will make you a bargain. I have a riddle for you. If you can answer it correctly, I will go away and leave you to eat your dinner in peace."

The wolf thought this might be a trick of some kind, but he was afraid to fight the bear. Besides that, he was very good at answering riddles. Making up riddles and answering them just happens to be a very popular game in the animal world. So, the wolf crouched on the ground nearby and nodded in agreement.

This was the bear's riddle:

"Sometimes it glitters, but often not;
May be cold, or may be hot!
Ever changing though the eye can't measure,
Concealed within are many treasures.
Some find safety beneath its gate,
While some may die beneath its weight!
Old and broken, it brings forth life.

"What is it, wolf?"

The wolf thought and thought. He repeated the lines to himself, and whenever he was not sure how they went, he made the bear repeat the whole thing to him again. In fact, he got so interested in the riddle he all but forgot the deer.

In the end, the bear had to say, "Come on, wolf! We don't have all night. Do you know the answer or don't you?"

The wolf's eyes lit up, and he cried out, "*Night!* That's it!

15

The night does all of those things. When the stars are out, it glitters. It may be cold or hot depending upon the season of the year. The night can get darker and darker, but after a time only an owl's sharp eyes can see any difference. Darkness hides everything, treasure or not. Some animals find safety in the night, but I kill others when the moon comes up. And, when the night is old and the sun breaks over the horizon, there is new life. The night! That is the answer!"

The outlaw bear nodded his wide head and said, "That is a very good answer, wolf. Very good indeed." Then, like a bolt of lightning, the bear hurled himself at the wolf and shouted, "But not good enough!"

Caught by surprise, the wolf was knocked over by one swipe of the bear's paw. When he got back on his feet, he turned and ran howling in fear and pain.

So, the outlaw bear ate the wolf's dinner, then went back to his den on the wild mountain and slept.

A few days later, as the bear was again wandering in the woods at the foot of the wild mountain, he smelled a very familiar and pleasant scent. Honey! And like all bears, he loved honey.

His nose took him to a hollow tree. There he saw bees flying in and out of a small knothole. He was just about to walk up to the tree and tear it open, when a small bee flew right in front of his nose and buzzed fiercely.

"Just where do you think you are going?" asked the bee, whose job it was to guard the hive.

"Why, to that tree, of course. I smell honey, and I just love to eat honey."

"What?" the bee cried. "That isn't your honey, bear. It

17

belongs to us. We have worked very hard to make it, gathering it from flowers all spring and summer. What gives you the right to take it from us?"

"The strength in my two strong paws is all the right that I have ever needed for anything, bee."

"If you try to take our honey, we will punish you, bear. We will sting you!"

The grizzly grinned at the little bee, showing his long fangs. "I have been stung before, bee, and getting my stomach full of honey is worth a little punishment from your kind." So, once again, he started to walk towards the tree.

The guard bee circled around the bear's head several times and again stopped in front of the grizzly's nose. Then, with the loudest noise he could make, he buzzed, "Wait, bear! Wait! Stop and think about what you are doing!"

"All right," the bear answered agreeably and sat down.

"What do you suppose would happen if all of the bears came down from the mountains and robbed every bee hive on the earth?"

"I don't know. What?" the outlaw bear asked with a shrug of his shaggy shoulders.

"Why all of the bees would die! We need this honey to live through the cold winters. And if all of the bees died and could not carry pollen between flowers in the spring, then all the plants would eventually die because there would be no seeds. And if all the plants died, all the animals that live off plants would die, and you grizzly bears live from hunting such animals. So, if they died, all you bears would starve too. Don't you see?"

The outlaw bear thought very hard about this. After a few moments, he replied, "I can see how that might happen, bee. But tell me, don't many plants live a long, long time?"

"Why, yes."

"Then all of this you described would take much longer than your lifetime and mine, wouldn't it, bee?"

"I suppose. But why should that matter?"

"Because, I don't care a whit about all the unborn bears in the universe. I only care about myself and what I can have in this life."

The bee became furious when he heard this. "How can you say such a terrible thing?" he asked. "If nature is to continue, every creature, great and small, must try to help the next generation of its kind."

Well, the bear laughed out loud at that. Then he said, "I don't think the loss of your little hive is going to make all those terrible things come true. There are many other bees and many other hives. But I tell you what, bee, I like to be fair. So, if you can answer a riddle I have, then I will go away and leave you in peace."

And the bear repeated his riddle:

"Sometimes it glitters, but often not;
May be cold, or may be hot!
Ever changing though the eye can't measure,
Concealed within are many treasures.
Some find safety beneath its gate,
While some may die beneath its weight!
Old and broken, it brings forth life.

"What is it, bee?"

The bee was stumped for the longest time by this riddle. (To tell you the truth, bees aren't very good at answering riddles. They seldom play any kind of game. Bees just work and build.) He buzzed around and around the bear's head in confusion, trying to figure out the answer. Then, it came to him in a flash, and he lighted on the end of the bear's nose.

"A river!" cried the bee. "That must be the answer! A river! If the moon or the sun is out, the water will glitter. It can be cold or hot. Beneath its surface, all kinds of changes take place, but the eye can't see them. Rivers conceal everything under them, treasure or not. Fish find safety under watery gates, while most of us would drown. And when a river becomes old and breaks into lakes, new forests spring up around its banks. The answer is a river."

The outlaw bear smiled at the little bee on the end of his nose and said quietly, "Very good, bee. Very good indeed. But I am afraid not good enough!" And the grizzly dropped his head so quickly that the bee fell from his nose. With a snap of his powerful jaws, he caught the tiny guard in mid-air and swallowed him.

Then the outlaw charged the tree. With all of his might, he tore at the bark until the tree split in half, and he ate all the honey inside. Of course, the bees tried to drive him away by stinging him, but the grizzly bear's hair and skin were so thick that they could only hurt the end of his nose and the soft spots around his eyes.The bear thought that was a very small price to pay for the good honey.

When he had finished eating, he cleaned himself in a nearby stream. Then he returned to his den on the wild mountain and slept again.

The next night, the outlaw grizzly bear was hungry for more meat. Down the mountain he trotted and into the woods. After a while he found that he was very near a log cabin where a man lived. Not too far from the cabin was a broad, open meadow. In the middle of that meadow was a flock of sheep. Now, the bear knew that sheep were no match for his strength and speed. So, he trotted out of the woods and across the meadow toward them. But before he could get close enough to charge the flock, he had to stop because a small dog suddenly appeared in his path and growled a warning.

"I cannot let you pass, bear," said the dog.

"Is that so?" the bear replied. "I am ten times your size and strength, dog. Do you really think you can stop me from killing a few of those sheep?"

"Probably not. But those sheep belong to my master, the man; and it is my duty to defend them from outlaws. I intend to do just that."

"You are very brave dog, braver than that wolf I met a few nights ago. But you are also a fool. If you fight me, I will kill you."

The dog did not seem frightened by this threat. He even took another step toward the bear and growled louder. "That may be so. But I will fight to save my master's sheep, even if it means my death. And there is something you need to think about, bear. If my master, the man, awakes in the morning to find me dead and his flock slaughtered, he will come after you. He will track you with my cousin, the hound, whose nose is keen as a wolf's. My cousin will remember my death, and he will not stop until he corners you. My master will chase you like

22

the wind itself on his horse with its thundering hooves, and he will have his rifle that can kill farther than our eyes can see. And although you might escape my master's anger for a while, outlaw bear, it will only be a matter of time before he catches you and punishes you for what you want to do tonight."

When the bear heard that, he sat down for the third time to think. In a little while, he replied, "I am an outlaw bear, and I have fought many times against many different animals, and I have never lost. So, I am not afraid of your master. But I will give you a fair chance, dog. I have a riddle, and if you can answer it I will leave you and your master's sheep alone."

The dog eyed the bear with suspicion and said, "Whether I can answer your riddle or not makes very little difference. If you attack my master's sheep, I will fight you, even if it means my death. But I would rather avoid the fight if I can, so give me your riddle." And the dog sat down.

The bear repeated his riddle for the third time:

> "Sometimes it glitters, but often not;
> May be cold, or may be hot!
> Ever changing though the eye can't measure,
> Concealed within are many treasures.
> Some find safety beneath its gate,
> While some may die beneath its weight!
> Old and broken, it brings forth life."

No sooner did the dog hear this riddle than he jumped to his feet and snapped, "You are trying to trick me, aren't you, bear? But it won't work."

23

"What do you mean, trick you?"

"You wouldn't have given me so easy a riddle if it was not a trick."

"No, dog. It is no trick. What is the answer?"

"A stone, of course! Anyone should know that. Some stones shine and some don't. At noonday they are hot and at midnight cold. Stones are always getting smaller from wind, heat, and water, but eyes can't measure the change because it is so slow. And they hide things that men find valuable like gold and silver. The badger finds safety beneath a stone, but a stone can also crush life. And when a stone is old and broken into tiny pieces, it becomes part of the soil that gives birth to trees and grass."

The outlaw bear, when he heard that answer, threw back his big head, opened his jaws, and laughed so loud that the flock of sheep ran toward the safety of their barn and a light came on inside the log cabin. The man was awake. He now knew of the bear's presence. But the brave sheep dog never budged an inch. He was ready to fight the grizzly if he took as much as one more step toward his master's sheep.

But the outlaw bear did not attack. He stood up, shook himself all over, and said with a flash of his long fangs, "You have answered correctly, dog. It is a stone. You are much smarter than those others. If I had given them the rest of their lives, they could never have come up with the simple answer to my riddle. The wolf was too blind to see it, and the bee was much too busy. I am good to my word. You and your master's sheep are safe."

And with those words, the outlaw bear turned on his heels and trotted back to the wild mountain, never to be seen again. Some animals say the grizzly did fear man. Others say he so respected the small dog for answering his riddle that he let that part of the country alone. Whatever the answer, it is enough that the outlaw bear did not return.

"The Riddle of the Outlaw Bear" and Real Life:

As there are outlaws in the animal world, so there are human outlaws—men and women who take whatever they want from others. They do not care if what they do is right or wrong or even if they hurt people, just as long as they get the things they are after.

The riddle a human outlaw asks is really much simpler than the bear's riddle. It goes like this: "If I am strong enough to take what I want, why shouldn't I?"

This story also suggests that some people in the world are like the wolf. Remember how he answered the bear's riddle? He said, "Night." Night is only the dark, which is really nothing at all. Men like the wolf believe there is no right or wrong. To them, there is no such thing as truth.

Most non-Christian people, however, are like the bee. They work and build and live very busy lives. But to them, truth is like water in a river. It flows along, winding around and around, changing directions as the years go by. Men like the bee believe in truth. They just believe that truth changes every so often..

But the Christian is like the shepherd's dog. Christians believe that truth is as solid as a stone because God is truth. And God says in the Bible that He will punish "outlaws" for their crimes. As the bear could not have escaped

25

the man, so a human outlaw cannot escape God, no matter how far or how fast he runs.

Romans 12:19—"Do not take revenge, my friends, but leave room for God's wrath, for it is written: 'It is mine to avenge; I will repay,' says the Lord."

How the Bobcat
Learned the Truth

Bobcats are "territorial" animals. That means they live and hunt in places they mark out very carefully. When one bobcat crosses a boundary line made by another and tries to hunt in that area, the result is often a fierce battle for ownership of the land.

Late one spring, a bobcat trotted out of the woods that surrounded a small lake the animals called Isom. Near the edge of the lake, he stopped suddenly. His nose told him that he was about to cross a boundary line set by another bobcat. (Bobcats make these lines with the odor from their bodies. You and I can't smell them, but those marks are as clear to another bobcat as a sign that tells us we are entering a town.)

27

The stranger sniffed deeply. He looked all around and listened for any sign of the Isom cat that lived in the region. Then, very silently he crossed the line and went down to the lake where he took a drink of water.

He was only there a few seconds before a young crow landed upon a branch several feet above his head and called to him, loudly. "Say there, stranger, are you lost? If you know what is good for you, you had better get away from here!"

The bobcat looked up at the bird and shook the drops of water from his whiskers. Then he said, very calmly, "No, I am not lost. And why should I leave this lake so soon. It is a very fine place."

"Doesn't your nose work?" asked the bird. "The land around this lake belongs to another bobcat. He is sure to find out that you are here, and he will come to fight you."

The stranger sat down and began to lick one of his paws. "My nose works just fine, crow. And as for a fight—well—we shall see about that in a little while. Tell me, crow, do you know much about this Isom cat?"

"No. I have only seen him a few times. But I have heard that he is very strong and he has done many great things."

"I would like to know more about this bobcat. Does he have any friends?"

"Why, yes, of course," the young crow replied.

"Then take me to one of them."

Crows are very curious birds by nature. The younger they are the more curious. They like to watch or hear strange things that they can repeat to their friends. So the young crow was happy to help the stranger. Off he flew

28

into the woods along the edge of the lake with the bobcat following him at a gallop.

A few moments later, the bird came to rest on the limb of a huge cottonwood tree. At the bottom of that tree was a hole dug under its thick roots. This was the den of an old fox.

The bobcat stopped outside the hole and purred loudly. A moment later, the red fox's head popped out of the hole. But when he saw that the sound was made by a stranger and not his friend the Isom cat, he quickly retreated.

"Don't be afraid," said the stranger. "I have only come to talk."

Slowly, the old fox crept back to the mouth of his den and again stuck his head out.

"I hear that you are a friend of the bobcat who lives in this territory."

"I know of him," the fox replied cautiously.

"That is not so," cried the young crow on the limb above them. "This fox is very old and doesn't hunt well anymore. The bobcat leaves him parts of his own meals. They are close friends."

"Ah," said the strange bobcat with a smile. "The truth! And that is all that I want to learn—the truth!"

"Why?" asked the fox.

"Because I may want to fight this Isom cat and take his land for myself!"

The young crow cawed with surprise and immediately flew to a lower branch. He did not want to miss a single word of the talk between the stranger and the fox.

The fox's eyes narrowed angrily at the stranger. He

said, "You do not want to try to take this land from my friend. He is too strong and too smart and too dangerous for you. He would beat you in a fight—maybe even kill you."

"Perhaps. Perhaps not," the bobcat purred back.

"Then listen to this," the fox snapped. "Not long ago, he hunted a wild pig and killed it on the far side of the lake. He is so strong that he dragged it to this very spot to share it with me. And you know how heavy those animals are. You have hunted them yourself. That is how strong he is. And to show you how smart he is, I have another story. Once, he was hunted by a pack of wild dogs, but he fooled them all. He led them into the swamps nearby where they became lost and were never seen again. And my friend is so dangerous that he has defended this land four times against other bobcats. He drove each of them away."

"Thank you," said the bobcat when he heard these things. Then he turned and walked away from the fox's den.

Of course, the young crow followed him. When they got back to the water's edge, the bird asked. "You are going to leave, aren't you?"

"No," was the bobcat's reply.

"But you heard what the fox said. The Isom bobcat has done many great things. He would beat you in a fight."

"Perhaps. Perhaps not. Tell me, crow, do you know an enemy of this bobcat?"

The young crow did not answer. He just flew into the woods with the stranger following him.

Finally, they reached a wide beaver dam. When the

31

strange bobcat trotted out of the woods, an old beaver who had been slapping mud into small cracks in the dam with his tail instantly jumped into the water and swam to his hut in the lake.

The beaver crawled on top of his stick-and-mud house and cried out, "Who are you?"

"I am a bobcat, of course," the stranger replied. "And I have come to challenge the Isom cat for control of this territory. I understand that you are his enemy."

"I am the enemy of all bobcats," the beaver shouted and gave a loud slap with his big, flat tail.

The young crow called out from a nearby tree, "But this beaver hates the Isom cat more than any other. They have been enemies for years."

"Ah," said the stranger. "The truth. And that is all I want to learn—the truth."

The bobcat trotted onto the beaver dam and sat down.

"I have heard that this Isom cat is very strong," he said to the beaver. "Once he killed a wild pig and dragged it many miles around this lake."

"Nonsense!" chattered the beaver. "He isn't so strong! That scrawny old pig probably didn't weigh as much as I do. And I'll bet he didn't carry it more than a hundred yards."

The bobcat carefully examined one of his big paws and said, "I also heard that he was hunted by a pack of wild dogs and was so smart that he led them into the swamps where they became lost and were never seen again."

The beaver slapped his tail in the water angrily. "Just talk and gossip! That was no great thing. Those were the smallest, thinnest, dumbest animals you ever saw. Not

one real dog among them. And I'll bet their noses were so bad they couldn't have tracked a skunk. It is no wonder the bobcat lost them in the swamps."

"And is it true that he has defended this land four times against other bobcats and has always won?" the stranger asked.

"Yes, that is so," said the beaver. "But those four were not like you. You can beat him easily. You are young and strong. He is growing old and weak. He is no match for you."

Just then, a loud cry echoed through the woods. It was the Isom bobcat. He had smelled the stranger and was coming to do battle.

The stranger slowly stood up, stretched himself all over, left the beaver dam, and trotted into the dark woods away from the sound of the Isom cat's war cry.

The young crow instantly flew after him. "Where are you going?" he asked. "Aren't you going to fight him?"

"No."

"But you heard what the beaver said," cried the bird. "You can beat him!"

The bobcat only paused long enough to give the young crow this answer. "The beaver wants us to fight. He hopes that we will kill or cripple each other. But this Isom bobcat is very strong and very smart and very fierce. I won't risk a fight with him.

"His enemy showed me that everything his friend said was true. You see, young crow, the fox might have lied for his friend. But when the beaver admitted that this bobcat had done all the great things the fox told me about, even though he made excuses, then I knew for certain that he had done all of those things. I learned the truth."

And with that the stranger ran into the woods away from the lake, because he knew the Isom bobcat would stop chasing him as soon as he crossed the border of his territory.

"How the Bobcat Learned the Truth" and Real Life:

Jesus of Nazareth said He was the Christ, the Messiah spoken of in the Old Testament, the Son of the living God sent into the world to save man from sin. To prove this, He did many great things we call *miracles*. He healed sick people just by touching them. He turned water into wine, made the dead come back to life, and fed thousands of men, women, and children with only five little loaves of bread and two fish. His friends told us about these great things and many others in the gospels of Matthew, Mark, Luke, and John.

Sometimes people who are not Christians say His friends lied. But Jesus had enemies too. They were the church leaders of the age in which He lived. They did not believe He was the Messiah, and they hated Him because so many people followed Him instead of them. Of course, the easiest way for them to prove He was not the Son of God was just to show that Jesus and His friends were liars and that Jesus never really did those miracles. But they could not. Too many people had watched Him do them. Even his enemies had seen them. So they had to admit that He had done all of the great things His friends wrote about, and all they could do was make up excuses.

35

Matthew 21:14-15—"The blind and the lame came to [Jesus] at the temple, and he healed them. But when the chief priests and the teachers of the law saw the wonderful things he did and the children shouting in the temple area, 'Hosanna to the Son of David,' they were indignant."

Matthew 12:22-24—"Then they brought Him a demon-possessed man . . . and Jesus healed him. . . . When the Pharisees heard this, they said, 'It is only by Beelzebub, the prince of demons, that this fellow drives out demons.' "

A Tale of Two Men

Deep in the woods of Canada there once lived a colony of beavers. Their home was a small valley surrounded by tall mountains. Three streams met in the valley, and the beavers built mud-and-stick dams to trap the water. As the years went by, they made the dams longer and wider, and the three streams kept bringing more and more water down the mountainsides until a lake was formed.

Finally, the lake grew so large that it took up most of the valley, and the number of beavers became so great that the whole day was filled with the slap-slap-slapping of their flat tails against the water and the noise of their sharp teeth gnawing on the bark of trees.

The beavers had lived in this place for so long that no animal in the woods could remember when or how the

37

first of their kind came to the valley. Even the black bear, the oldest creature in that part of the forest, could not re-call the first beavers who arrived. But the bear knew many strange stories. One of those stories said the first beavers were brought to the valley by a man who lived in a cabin very close to the lake. The bear claimed that long ago the man planted the trees that grew in the valley—the trees that the beavers used for food and to build their houses and dams. Then the man brought the first beavers to the valley so they could build the lake.

That story always made the beavers angry. They hated the man. They blamed him for all of their troubles. And they hated the old black bear too, not only for telling that story, but also because he liked the man and always said the man was a friend to all the animals in the forest.

But the beavers did not believe the man was their friend. They said he was their enemy, and they wanted to be rid of him. They remembered a long, hot summer years earlier when the three streams nearly dried up. Many beavers had to leave their homes, because the lake water got so low it left their huts on dry land. When the heat was at its worst, the man came. He walked onto one of their dams with a pick and a shovel. He broke it! And even more of their precious water escaped through the hole he made.

The beavers remembered how the man often came into the woods with his long axe and cut down trees. And with so many beavers living in the lake, there were just no trees to spare.

The beavers recalled how the man once caught twelve of their kind in nets. He put them in cages and carried them away. The rest of the beaver colony gave them up for lost, but, weeks later, one of the twelve crawled out of the woods. He was thin and very tired. He said the man had carried him and the other eleven beavers far, far away. He set them free in another mountain valley. There was plenty of food there and a deep stream where they could swim. But it was a hard place. The new valley was dark and frightening. The water was cold. He missed his friends and wanted to go home, but the others were afraid of the woods. The other eleven beavers remained in the dark valley and started building dams and huts and gathering food for the winter. But he left. He wandered alone in the woods and went through many dangers before he found his friends and family again.

In a way, those twelve beavers were lucky. The nets and the cages had not hurt them. There were other traps around the lake that caught beavers. These were made of cruel iron. They had jaws like a hungry wolf. When they snapped shut on a beaver, they killed him. Even though the beavers were very, very careful, these iron traps were hidden in places they never expected. So, many of their kind had been murdered by the awful iron traps over the years.

Yes. They hated the man. They blamed him for all those troubles and many more.

Then, one day, everything changed.

There was a young beaver all the rest of the colony loved. He was very kind and helpful. One night as he was wandering along the edge of the lake—SNAP!—one of the cruel iron traps caught him. All of his friends came to help, but it was too late.

39

The next morning, the man came. He took their friend out of the trap, threw the young beaver across one shoulder, and carried him away.

That very afternoon, the beavers held a council. There was much angry slapping of tails on the water and clattering of long teeth. They wanted to do something about the man. Anything! The beavers made so much noise that the old black bear, who had been eating berries nearby, came to the water's edge to see what was the trouble.

He walked onto one of the beavers' dams and started to ask what was happening, but as soon as the beavers saw him, they began to make so much noise the old black bear could not understand a thing they said. The beavers hissed and grunted and clattered their teeth and slapped their tails. Oh, how angry they were when they saw the bear who said the man was a friend to all the animals in the woods. Two or three of the younger beavers swam close to the bear and splashed water on him by flipping their flat tails.

When things calmed down enough for the bear to make himself heard above all the noise, he asked, "What is the matter with all of you? Why are you angry at me? I have done you no harm."

The leader of the beaver colony had been sitting on top of his hut in the center of the lake. Now he jumped into the water, swam to the dam, and crawled up right in front of the old bear.

The leader of the beavers snarled angrily. "You say the man brought the first beavers to this valley. You say he is a friend of all the animals in the forest. That is a lie! He is our enemy! He is cruel and terrible! He is the cause of all

of our troubles. We need to be rid of him!"

The old bear shook the water from his fur and said calmly, "I never lied to you. My mother told me the story of how the man brought the first beavers to this valley long ago. I still believe it. And the man has always been a friend of mine. He is your friend too."

"*Liar!*" the beaver shouted. He jumped at the bear and tried to bite him. The black bear backed up quickly, so the beaver just missed him. The bear stepped off the dam onto the shore of the lake, where he knew the beaver would not follow him.

"The man is no friend of ours," the beaver cried. "Look at all of his terrible crimes against us. You remember the summer when there was no rain. He came and broke our dam and let water escape. There was very little left. What do you have to say about that, bear? Was the man being a friend of the beavers when he broke our dam?"

The old black bear snorted back, "I said he was a friend to all of the animals. If there was only a little water in your lake, how much less do you think was below your valley? The man broke your dam to help other creatures in the forest. Other animals besides beavers need water to live!"

Around the lake, beaver tails began slapping the water. They did not like the bear's answer at all. They did not think they should have to suffer to help any other animal.

"The man cuts down our trees with his long axe," said the leader. "And there is only a little food left for us to eat."

"But the man planted the trees in this valley. Surely he has a right to some of them," the bear answered.

"If he did, then he did not plant enough of them. If he

42

was really a friend of beavers, as you say, then he would have seen to it that there was food enough for us to live in this valley forever and not go hungry."

There was a clatter of teeth as the other beavers agreed with their leader.

Another beaver hopped into the water and swam to the dam. He sat up in front of his leader and snapped, "Is the man my friend too, bear? He caught a dozen of us in nets and carried us far away from our friends and our families. He put us in a cold, lonely valley. All of the others are still there. But I escaped! I came back to my home through many dangers. Is he a friend of mine?"

Now, it was the bear's turn to get angry. He growled at the new beaver on the dam. "You blame the man for troubles you make yourselves. Open your eyes! There are too many of your kind in this lake. You have cut down too many trees and grown fat. Don't blame my friend the man because you eat too much. When he caught you in his nets, he was probably just trying to help you. He brought the first of your kind to this valley. Perhaps he took you and your eleven friends to another valley where you could safely build another lake even better than this one."

At that, all the beavers around the lake began shouting and jumping in and out of the water, clattering their teeth and throwing mud and sticks into the air with their tails. Oh, how angry they were. They were sure that no other lake could be as beautiful as their own.

Finally, the leader got them quiet again. He waddled past the other beaver and came to the end of the dam, where he was just a few inches from the bear.

43

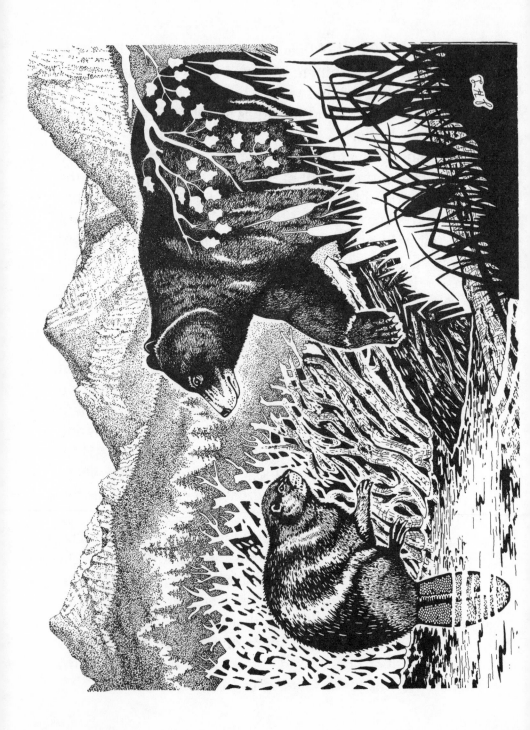

"A friend of the beavers," he snapped. "You are a fool, bear. If all of your answers were true—and I don't believe any of them—then tell me this. The man has more than nets around our lake. He has iron traps hidden everywhere. They snap shut like the jaws of a wolf. They kill our friends. Does he set these traps for us because he is our friend?"

"Those are not his traps," answered the bear. "There are two men in these woods, not just one."

Instantly, the lake became very still. The beavers were so surprised by this answer they could not move or make a sound.

Finally, their leader asked, "What do you mean, bear? There is only one man. He is the only one we have seen."

"No. There are two men. One lives near the lake. The other man lives below these mountains and comes here with his iron traps and sets them for your friends."

"I don't believe you, bear!"

"Then believe this!" said the bear, and he raised his right paw. Around the leg was a wide scar where no hair grew. "The man of traps caught me long ago. I would have died if the man of the lake had not found me. At first I was afraid of him. I fought him. But he tied me with his nets. Then, he took the iron trap off my leg and set me free. He went through the woods looking for bear traps. And whenever he found one, he took a tree branch and stuck it in the iron jaws so the trap could not hurt me.

"From that day on, I stayed near the man of the lake. He is stronger than the other man. The man of traps is afraid of him. As long as I am close to my friend's cabin, the man of traps will not come near me."

45

"I don't believe you," said the leader of the beavers. "How do you know it was not your friend who set the iron trap for you?"

"Because he set me free! Why would he trap me just to set me free?"

Once again the beavers became angry. "If that is true," they began to cry, "if the man of the lake is stronger than the other, then he should break all the traps in the forest. He should chase the man of traps away. Why doesn't he do that? Why does he let us suffer?"

The old black bear just shook his head slowly from side to side. "I am a bear, not a man. I don't know why men do all the things that they do."

The leader of the beaver colony dug his flat tail into the mud of the dam and slung it right into the old black bear's face. Instantly, all the other beavers swam to the bank and began doing the same thing, tossing mud and sticks at the bear and splashing water on him.

Finally, the old bear turned and walked into the woods.

"Go away! Go away!" they shouted after him. "There is only one man. He is our enemy!"

After a long while the beavers calmed down and began to talk about what they should do. They knew they could not hurt the man or stop him from setting traps. So, they made the hardest decision of their lives. They agreed, one and all, that they should leave their beautiful lake to escape the man.

That night, they divided into three groups. Each of the groups chose a different stream and began following it. They would look for new homes. It took many days for the three groups of beavers to find new valleys. But when they did, they began building dams and huts and gathering food for the winter.

They were very sad about leaving their beautiful lake. But they were happy to escape the man. They made up songs about how good it was to be free of him.

It did not take them long to discover how wrong they were. In no time at all, more iron traps appeared around all three new valleys.

"We are not far enough from the man of the lake!" the beavers cried.

Again they moved. But it was no use. Wherever they went, sooner or later the iron traps appeared and caught more beavers, even more than were caught around their first home.

For, you see, the beavers had made a terrible mistake. To them all men looked the same. But there were two men, not just one. One was a farmer and a woodsman. He loved the animals and wanted to help them. The other was a trapper. With his iron traps, he killed animals for their fur. And whenever the beavers moved, he would follow them. He set more and more traps because he knew that the farther the beavers moved from the woodsman, the safer his traps would be. The woodsman could not find them and break them.

But the old black bear lived in peace. He stayed close to the woodsman's cabin, and the woodsman never let the trapper hurt him again.

"A Tale of Two Men" and Real Life:

If you talk to your friends about God, sooner or later one of them may say, "But God is cruel. He allows sickness and death. I can't believe in a God who is so cruel and terrible."

People like to blame God for everything that goes wrong in the world, just as the beavers blamed the man of the lake for everything bad that happened to them.

First, the beavers did not want to admit how much the woodsman had done for them. He placed them in the mountain valley in the first place. He planted the trees they used for food and building. When there were too many beavers in the lake, he helped by taking a dozen of them to another valley.

God put man on the earth. He loves man. He provides man's food and the things man needs to work and build.

Psalm 104:14 says, "He makes grass grow for the cattle, and plants for man to cultivate—bringing forth food from the earth."

Second, the beavers blamed the man for many troubles they created themselves. They cut down too many trees, without thinking of what they would need later. They got angry at the man for breaking a hole in their dam, but their dam was keeping water from other animals who were suffering more than they were.

Many men blame God for troubles that they create themselves. And they get angry at Him when He has to take something from them in order to help other people. They are selfish.

But, of course, the most important answer the black bear gave to the beavers was that there were two men. One was good. The other was bad.

God has an enemy. His name is Satan. He is a terrible power, and he not only hates God, he also hates man.

First Peter 5:8 reads, "Your enemy the devil prowls around like a roaring lion looking for someone to devour."

As the trapper caught the old black bear in one of his terrible iron traps, so Satan traps men in their sin. But God can set people free, as the woodsman set the black bear free. God sent His only Son, Jesus, to die for our sins and set us free from the trap Satan holds us in.

One day, God will defeat Satan completely. Why God is waiting to do that, no one can really say for sure, no more than the black bear knew why the woodsman did not spring all the traps around the lake. We cannot always know why God does things the way that He does them. The Bible says, "My thoughts are not your thoughts, neither are your ways my ways, declares the Lord" (Isaiah 55:8).

Finally, the beavers believed that if they simply escaped the woodsman, their troubles would be over. But the trapper followed them. People have often thought that if they could just get far enough away from God, they could build a better world. But troubles have always followed them, because of the cruel power of Satan.

Christians should remember what Jesus told them: "In this world, you will have trouble. But take heart! I have overcome the world" (John 16:33).

Wind and Water

Animals are like people in many ways. For one thing, they must learn from what happens to them every day. Many are curious about everything that goes on around them. They keep their eyes and ears open, and they learn quickly. But other animals are only interested in something to help them live and eat.

There was once a young squirrel who lived in a hollow at the top of an old oak tree. He was very curious about the world outside his little nest. It was full of bright colors and strange sounds and new smells. He was too little to help his parents gather nuts, but whenever they were away for a long time, he liked to slip outside, scurry down the oak tree to the ground, and explore the woods around his home.

One summer afternoon, the young squirrel's wandering took him to the edge of a river not too far from his oak tree. It was a very hot day, and he was terribly thirsty. So he hopped onto a fallen tree, which lay partly on the bank and partly in the water, and crept along that log towards the river.

But just about the time the little squirrel reached the spot where the swift water rippled over the end of the log, something happened that terrified him. A colorful big butterfly fluttered past his head and over the surface of the river. Suddenly, the water under the butterfly rolled and boiled. A strange beast, the likes of which the young squirrel had never seen or imagined, leaped into the air. It was long and thin. Its silver skin sparkled in the bright sunlight. It had great, round, yellow eyes and a huge mouth. It swallowed the big butterfly whole. When its jaws snapped shut, the silver creature fell into the water with a loud flop and a great splash and disappeared.

The little squirrel looked all around in alarm. Everything had happened so fast. One second the colorful butterfly was there. The next it was gone. Then, the squirrel thought, *What if that big shiny creature comes back and wants to swallow me?* So, he turned and ran to his nest in the top of the old oak tree as fast as his little paws would carry him. He hid under the dry grass and leaves his parents had gathered to make his bed.

It was a long time before he found the courage to crawl to the small hole that was the door of his home and peek outside. He watched for the big shiny creature. Any moment, he expected to see it climbing up the trunk of his oak tree, trying to reach his nest and eat him. But it was nowhere to be seen.

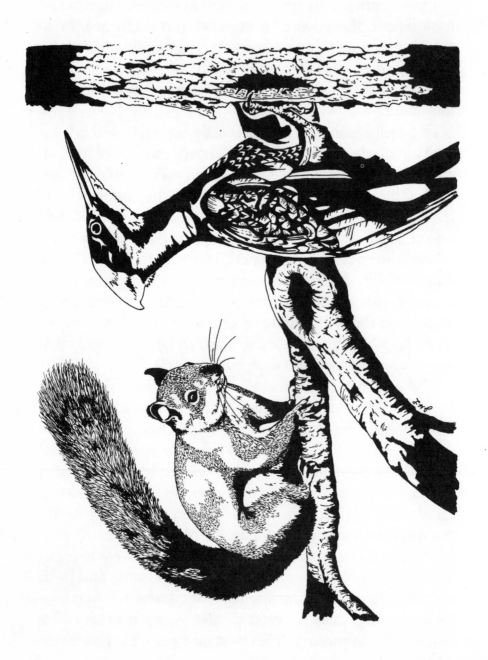

He sat there for a long time, watching and waiting. But nothing happened. Finally, the little squirrel started thinking.

Maybe that big shiny creature can't climb trees, he said to himself. *Maybe it can't even crawl out of the river like a turtle or a frog. It may live under the water and only come up when it's hungry for butterflies!*

Just then, there came a tap-tap-tapping on the side of the oak tree. The little squirrel scampered out of his hole and down the side of the tree to the nearest limb. He found a big woodpecker chipping away at the bark of the oak with his long black beak, searching for bugs to eat.

Now, there is something you should know about woodpeckers. They aren't curious about anything that doesn't have to do with trees or bugs or the winds that carry them when they fly. They stay busy all of the time. They hate being bothered when they are hungry, and sometimes they can be really grumpy.

The woodpecker that the little squirrel found tapping away at the trunk of his oak tree was very old, very busy, very hungry, and very grumpy.

"Excuse me, Mr. Woodpecker!" the squirrel said. But the bird kept pecking away at the bark of the tree without answering him.

So, the young squirrel crept closer. "Excuse me, Mr. Woodpecker!" he chattered again, this time much louder. He heard a grumble from the bird, but that was all.

The woodpecker kept chipping away at the bark until he uncovered a small black bug and gobbled it down.

The young squirrel decided that this woodpecker must be deaf. So, he ran right up to the bird, put his mouth to the woodpecker's ear, and shouted as loud as he could.

"EXCUSE ME, MR. WOODPECKER!"

That did the trick. The bird was so startled by the squirrel's shout that he dropped a fat beetle he had just found hiding beneath the bark and flew halfway to the next tree in fright. Oh, how angry he was when he looked over his wing and saw the young squirrel staring after him. The woodpecker turned in mid-air and darted back to the oak tree. He landed on a limb right in front of the squirrel and cried loudly, "What is the matter with you? Why are you shouting at me, you silly little squirrel?"

"I thought you were deaf," the young squirrel said.

"Well, I wasn't until you screamed in my ear!" the woodpecker chirped angrily. "What do you want? Can't you see that I'm much too busy to be bothered by you!"

"But something happened at the river today that frightened me. I want you to tell me what it was."

The bird just grunted loudly and flew back to the trunk of the oak tree where he again started to peck at the bark. "I don't have any time—" tap, tap, tap "—to talk to you—" tap, tap "—about things you can't understand. Why you are just a young squirrel—" tap, tap, tap "—everything frightens you."

But the little squirrel would not let him alone. He crept closer to the bird and chattered, "There is a big shiny creature that lives under the river. What is it?"

"Nonsense—" tap, tap, tap "—nothing lives under the river," the woodpecker replied.

"But I saw it!"

"Silly stuff! Nonsense—" tap, tap "—you didn't see any such thing."

"Yes, I did," the young squirrel barked. "It jumped right out of the river and ate a big bright butterfly!"

"You probably saw something fall out of a tree and land in the water," the woodpecker said. "And a frog ate that butterfly, I'll bet."

The squirrel got so angry he stamped his little paws up and down on the limb and cried, "You are wrong! You are wrong! I saw it happen! Something big and shiny does live under the river, and it jumps up and eats butterflies!"

"Nothing lives under the river, you silly squirrel. And since you won't leave me alone, it looks like I will have to show you why."

So, down the woodpecker flew to the edge of the river, and the young squirrel scampered after him.

When the little squirrel reached the tree that was lying partly in the river and partly on the bank, he turned to the woodpecker and started to tell him where he saw the big shiny creature jump out of the water. But before he could open his mouth, the bird swooped down and pecked him right on top of the head.

"Ouch!" the squirrel cried. "Why did you do that?"

"You want to know why nothing lives under the river. I am going to show you." And the woodpecker flew by him and—*whack*—pecked him on the head again.

"Ouch! Ouch!" the young squirrel piped and scurried backwards until his paws touched the swift water that was rolling over the bark of the fallen tree.

The woodpecker landed on the log right in front of the little squirrel and asked, "Do turtles or frogs or snakes live under the river? Of course not. They live on the river bank. And do you know why?"

But the little squirrel was too busy rubbing his sore head to answer.

"Well then, I'll show you why!" said the bird, and he hopped forward and pecked the squirrel once more.

"Ouch! Ouch! Ouch!" yelled the little squirrel and he jumped away from the bird and—*plop*—fell into the river.

The swift river current dragged him under immediately. His mouth and nose and eyes and ears filled with water. When he bobbed back to the surface of the river, he coughed and sputtered.

Squirrels live in trees, so they aren't very good swimmers. But they have quick legs, and they use their heads whenever they are in danger. The little squirrel kept paddling his paws as fast as he could, and he was able to stay on top of the water so he would not drown. And as soon as the swift river current carried him under the branches of a cypress tree, he reached out and grabbed one and pulled himself to safety.

He looked and sounded terrible. His fur was soaking wet. He was sneezing and coughing from the water in his nose and throat, and he was shaking all over from fear.

The woodpecker flew to a nearby branch and said, "There. Let that be a lesson to you! Now, you know why there is no big shiny animal living under the river. Because, if it did live down there, it would have to breathe water. And nothing can breathe water!

"Turtles and frogs and snakes swim under the water, but, sooner or later, they must come up for air. Fresh air. The air that I fly through each day. So, you really didn't see a big shiny creature jump out of the river and swallow a butterfly. It was all your imagination."

The little squirrel had got his breath back by that time, and he was angry. He saw a cypress seed hanging near his head, and he grabbed it and threw it just as hard as he could at the woodpecker. Now, the little squirrel was very good at tossing acorns, so the cypress seed landed squarely between the bird's eyes.

The woodpecker squawked loudly and flew away crying, "That will teach me never to help a squirrel. Shiny creatures that live under water. Silly stuff! Nonsense! Nonsense! Nonsense!" And the bird disappeared into the woods.

The little squirrel finally stopped shaking and was just about to crawl out of the cypress tree and return to his nest when a voice whistled at him from below. "Don't you know that squirrels are supposed to live in trees!"

At the foot of the cypress tree stood a large, brown otter. He was standing on his hind legs staring curiously at the little squirrel and whistling in the good-natured way otters do when they think something is funny. And the young squirrel, all wet and mad, did look a little funny.

The squirrel had never seen an otter before, so he asked, "What are you?"

"I am an otter," the animal replied. "And I live in the river, but if all the squirrels in these woods start swimming there won't be any room for me, and I guess that I will have to learn how to climb trees." And the otter whistled very high and loud, which is the same as laughing in otter language.

"That mean old woodpecker chased me into the river," the young squirrel replied.

"What on earth for?"

"He was trying to show me that I couldn't breathe water."

The otter whistled again. He really thought that was funny. "It seems to me a squirrel could learn something as simple as that without getting half-drowned."

"Oh, the woodpecker wasn't just talking about squirrels. He was showing me that nothing can live under the river, because every animal has to breathe air." And the young squirrel told the otter how the shiny creature had frightened him when it jumped out of the water and swallowed the butterfly.

"But I guess I just imagined all that," the squirrel finally said. "The woodpecker must be right. Nothing can breathe water."

Well, when the otter heard that he started whistling and whistling in his otter laugh and running up and down the river bank playfully.

The little squirrel became angry again. "What is the matter with you?" he barked.

"This is the funniest thing I've ever heard in my life. What a silly little squirrel you are."

"I am not silly. And I don't see a thing funny about all of this!"

The otter jumped to his feet and said, "I do. And if you will stay on that limb a few moments more, I can show you why."

Then, the otter jumped into the river and disappeared under the water. Well, the young squirrel decided to wait for him. In a little while, the otter's head popped up and he had something in his mouth.

The otter swam to the bank. He dropped the thing on

the ground beneath the cypress tree, so the little squirrel could see it, and held it with his front paws. It was long and silver colored and shiny, and it had big, round, yellow eyes. On one end was a wide mouth and on the other was a broad, flat tail that flapped from side to side furiously. It looked just like the silver creature that jumped out of the water and swallowed the butterfly, but it was much smaller.

"It is called a fish," said the otter. "They are born and live and die under water. They can't stay on dry land for long because they don't breathe air the way you and I do. And big fish sometimes jump out of the water and eat butterflies that get too close to the river.

"Now do you see why you are such a silly little squirrel? You wanted to learn something about the river so you went to a bird, who studies only the wind. All that an old woodpecker can tell you about the river is what he sees when he flies over it. And he never sees much, because he is always busy thinking about trees and bugs. If you wanted to know something about water, you should have asked an animal that lives in the water, an animal like me."

Of course, otters eat fish, and by this time the otter was getting hungry. So, he whistled loudly, picked up the fish he had caught, and swam away.

The young squirrel returned to his nest in the old oak tree. He had learned a very important lesson that summer afternoon.

"Wind and Water" and Real Life:
People always have questions about God. The trouble

is, they are sometimes like the young squirrel—they try to get answers from the wrong people. For example, they go to a scientist and ask him whether or not there is a God. But one who studies only science honestly cannot tell them, because a scientist does not study about God or angels or Satan. That is not his job. He studies the laws of nature, the rules that belong to man's world. Those rules tell us important facts that we need to know, like how the earth, moon, stars, and planets go around one another, and how plants and animals grow, and how the weather changes, and so on.

But God is not ruled by the same laws that rule men. The world where He lives is not at all like ours. It is controlled by a completely different set of rules. They are so different from the laws of our world that men who study God give His world a name—"the supernatural." That word just means above and beyond the laws of nature.

Just to show you how different God's world is from our own—nothing grows old there, because there is no such thing as time. Peter wrote, "Do not forget this one thing, dear friends: With the Lord a day is like a thousand years, and a thousand years are like a day" (2 Peter 3:8).

Now, if you have a question about a car, would you ask somebody who studies turtles? Of course not. You should ask a person who studies cars, a mechanic.

So, if you want to learn about the laws of nature, you should go to someone who knows the laws of nature. But if you want to learn about God, go to someone who knows about God's supernatural world.

The little squirrel tried to learn about the river from a

bird. But he got the wrong answer. It took the otter to show him the truth.

1 Corinthians 2:14—"The man without the Spirit does not accept the things that come from the Spirit of God, for they are foolishness to him, and he cannot understand them, because they are spiritually discerned."

Tracks in the Snow

Long before the outlaw bear came down from his den on the wild mountain and told his riddle to the wolf, the bee, and the shepherd's dog, the American West was ruled by animals who saw men only now and then. In fact, some of the sure-footed creatures like the bighorn sheep, the wild mountain goats, and the deer knew nothing at all about men because they lived away up on the slopes of the Rocky Mountains. The cliffs were so high and the paths so steep that Indians and mountain men and explorers passed through their part of the country very few times. That is why the tracks that the animals found one morning caused so much excitement.

A great snowstorm had covered the mountains with a blanket of white. When the animals came out of hiding, they found the strange tracks across a wide, flat meadow.

Footprints! But these footprints were not like any tracks left by creatures they knew.

In no time at all, most of the deer and bighorn sheep who lived near the meadow were gathered around them.

"What kind of animal could make tracks like these?" asked the buck who was king of the deer herd.

"I don't know," said a bighorn ram, shaking his huge horns from side to side. "But they were not made by an animal who lives on this mountain. I think whatever made these tracks walks on two legs!"

That caused a terrible stir among the other animals, because the only creature they knew that stood on two legs was the bear. But no bear could walk across the meadow on his back legs. It was much too wide.

So, the animals stood in the meadow for a long time, talking and talking. It was a great mystery. They might have stayed there until the blowing snow finally covered the tracks completely, if the mountain goat had not bounded down from the rocky cliffs above them.

"What is the matter with all of you?" the goat cried from the top of a huge boulder. "Why are you standing in this meadow?"

It did not take long for the others to tell him what they had found. The goat snorted loudly, jumped into the snow, and crossed the meadow to see the strange tracks.

All the other animals were very interested in what the mountain goat would say. They knew he was very smart. He had to be. He lived at the very top of the mountains where the eagles built their nests, and he climbed on paths that no other animal was sure-footed enough to use or smart enough even to find.

The mountain goat looked at the tracks in the snow for only a second or two. Then, he raised his white head so his nose was stuck way up in the air, closed both eyes, and tried to look very important in front of the other animals.

"A moose," he said.

"What?" asked the king of the deer herd.

"I said that a moose made these tracks!" replied the goat.

"What on earth is a moose?" asked one of the bighorn sheep.

"It is a huge beast with great, wide horns and a long, ugly head," said the goat, who was very proud of himself because he knew something that the other animals did not. "I met one last year. I found his tracks in the snow. They were so strange that I followed them down the mountainside until I caught up with him. The moose told me all about his kind and how they live near the lakes below our mountains."

Then, the goat began to talk and talk and talk about the moose. He told the other animals what the moose said he liked to eat and where he lived and all about his strange habits.

Of course, the other animals got awfully tired of listening to the goat. But they were polite and did not interrupt. After all, the goat was very smart, and he had a way of making everything he said sound so important.

When he finally stopped talking, the ram who was the leader of the bighorn sheep herd asked, "But does a moose walk on two legs?"

"Of course not," answered the goat.

"Then I don't think a moose made these tracks. It looks to me like these footprints were left by something that walks on two legs."

"Impossible!" the goat cried. "Nothing could walk that far on two legs. I told you what made these tracks. A moose!"

The ram just shook his head slowly from side to side. "You followed one strange track in the snow to the end and found a moose. But that doesn't mean this track was made by one. It seems to me the only way to be certain what is at the end of this trail is to follow it."

The goat snorted loudly. "You sheep are so stupid! I don't have the time to follow every strange track I find in the snow. One was enough." Then, he began to hop back up the rocky cliff above the meadow, and every few steps he would turn around and cry, "A moose!"

After he was gone, the ram said, "I don't care what that old goat says, the animal that made these tracks walks on two legs. I'm sure of it!"

The king of the deer herd replied, "I don't know. The mountain goat is very smart. He lives far above us on the mountaintop, and he can see for many, many miles. If he says a moose made these tracks, he is probably right."

The ram pawed the snow angrily. "I know one thing about mountain goats—once they get an idea in their heads, an avalanche couldn't knock it out. I'm going to follow these tracks."

"And I'll go with you," the deer king said. "The goat is probably right. But I have never seen a moose, and I would like to talk to one."

So, off they ran across the meadow and into the

woods. The trail went on for miles. It took them down the mountainside to a deep valley where the snow was light and the ground very hard and covered with stones. Of course, the wind blew all the time, and it whipped the snow around and around in great clouds.

As the hours passed by, the snow began to cover the footprints, and the ram and the deer found it harder and harder to follow the tracks. Finally, the trail in the valley disappeared completely.

They searched for more than an hour but found nothing. They were about to give up and return to the mountain meadow when the ram's sharp eyes spotted the footprints again. Only a few were left. They were at the mouth of a small cave. Pine trees around the cave kept the blowing snow from covering them.

The ram was short enough to get his head and shoulders into the little cave. But he saw that inside it was blocked with stones and pieces of wood.

He stepped back and said, "If this moose is as large as the goat says, I don't see how he could have got into a cave so small. And besides that, whatever went into that cave covered itself up with sticks and stones. It acts more like a mole than a moose."

Once again, the deer replied, "I don't know. The mountain goat is very smart. If he says the tracks were made by a moose, they probably were. Maybe there are little moose that sleep in caves. I think we should call and try to wake it up."

"All right," the ram agreed. "Something is there. I can smell it. And we have come too far to go back without an answer."

So, the ram and the deer stamped and bellowed and snorted and challenged. But nothing came out of the cave.

"What should we do now?" asked the ram.

"You can stop making all that noise, that's what you can do!" cried an angry voice. And out of a hole a few feet from them popped a badger.

Now, badgers live in the ground. They are short, wide animals with flat heads, small ears and eyes, and very strong legs, which are just perfect for digging. They sleep all day and come out at night to search for food.

It was late afternoon when the ram and the deer woke this mother badger up, but it would still be hours before she went out looking for breakfast. She was angry, and so were her two little cubs. The three of them waddled out of their home with every hair standing on end (badgers do that when they get frightened or angry), and it made them look twice their real sizes.

"I'm sorry," the deer apologized. "There is a moose in this little cave, and we are trying to make him come out."

Even the little badger cubs laughed when they heard that. They lived in the valley and had seen many moose. "That is the silliest thing I have ever heard," the she-badger said. "A moose can't crawl into a hole. Its legs are too long and its horns too wide."

"I told you!" said the ram.

The deer felt very bad, because he had so wanted to talk to a moose.

The badger family crawled into the cave and sniffed the pile of stones. Then, they got very excited. The mother badger cried, "I don't know what has been here, but there is food hidden behind these sticks and stones!"

So, the three badgers began digging as hard as they could, because the smell of food made them terribly hungry. And when a badger is hungry and looking for food, it can dig faster and harder than you can imagine. Rocks, branches, snow, and ice flew out of the cave's mouth. In a few moments, the badgers dug a tunnel into the back of the little cave and began to drag out all kinds of packages of every shape and color. Inside one package they found dried meat and beans. In another, there was a strange-smelling powder stuffed into the horn of a buffalo. And the biggest package of all contained something made from wood and metal. It was very long and oddly shaped. It was coated in a foul-smelling oil. None of them could imagine what it was or why all these things were hidden in the cave. But the hungry badgers wasted no time with questions. They just ate the dried meat and the beans while the ram and the deer sniffed nervously at the long thing made of wood and metal.

Now, I am sure you have already guessed what the animals had found. It was a "cache," a hiding place used by men for food and tools. Early that morning, a mountain man had crossed the snow-covered meadow. When he got to the valley, he found the little cave. Inside it, he stored food, and gunpowder in a buffalo's horn, and a rifle. If he ever needed them, he would come back and dig them out.

Well, it did not take the badger cubs long to find out that the rifle had moving parts. Just as soon as they finished eating the dried meat and beans, they began to play with it. They chewed on the wood. They pulled the hammer back until it locked. They opened the little cover in the rifle butt, and underneath it they discovered a little nook where round, lead musket balls were kept. The cubs took them out, one at a time, and rolled them in the snow. Then, it happened!

One of the cubs discovered the rifle's trigger. He tugged at it with one of his paws, and suddenly the hammer fell. There was a flash of fire, a small puff of smoke, and the rifle exploded.

What a terrible noise it made! The sound echoed from the walls of the valley and shook the snow from the pine trees. The rocky ground in front of the little cave trembled.

The animals were very lucky that none of them got hurt. But you can imagine how frightened they were. The badgers scurried to their hole and ducked inside as quick as lightning. The ram and the deer ran up the mountain-side as fast as they could and never once looked back until they reached the flat meadow where they had first seen the strange tracks.

Of course, they told all the animals on the mountain what had happened. Then, they made up a song, and whenever they saw the mountain goat climbing on the cliffs above them, they sang it as loud as they could:

"The mountain goat is such a silly old goose;
    Wherever he looks, he sees a moose.
In the water or in the snow,
    He finds them hiding high and low.
He lives on the cliffs so very high
    That he sees the world through different eyes.
From way up there its all so plain,

74

That every trail must end the same.
Two legs, four legs, six legs, ten,
   Big as a tree or small as a hen,
No need to fear what's on the loose,
   For in the end, it will be a moose!"

"Tracks in the Snow" and Real Life:

There are people who want you to believe that there is no God because, once upon a time, they heard someone say something about God that turned out not to be true. A person may have told them they saw God do this or that. But, when they went and looked for themselves, it was not God at all. The person only saw something happen that he could not understand, and he thought that God caused it. But really, he was wrong. Now, whenever these people hear that anyone has seen God do something, they refuse to believe him.

They may say something like this to you. "Long ago, men saw God in everything from storms to earthquakes. But now, science has shown us that these things happen naturally. So, whatever you hear about God's miracles is really not true. They can all be explained by science."

When you hear that, just remember the song that the other animals made up about the mountain goat, because people who talk that way are as silly as he was. The mountain goat followed one strange track in the snow to the end and found a moose. After that, whenever he saw a strange trail in the snow, he always thought it was made by a moose, no matter how different it looked.

But the ram's answer was right. The only way to know

75

what is at the end of a trail is to follow it. Just because one group of strange footprints turned out to be made by a moose doesn't mean that all strange trails were left by one.

Since Bible days, God has done all kinds of wonderful things for people. Many books have been written by different men about these acts of God in their lives. The special things God has done for His people are some of the "trails" God leaves for man. They show how real and how strong He is.

Non-Christians would try to make you believe ten thousand stories of God's miracles are not true because a dozen other stories turned out to be lies. That is the reason "the mountain goat is such a silly old goose; wherever he looks, he sees a moose."

Psalm 40:5 — "Many, O Lord my God are the wonders you have done. The things you planned for us no one can recount to you; were I to speak and tell of them, they would be too many to declare."

How Water Ran Uphill

Along the Mississippi River in the northwest corner of Tennessee is a large lake called Reelfoot. It was created early in the 1800s by powerful earthquakes. They shook the earth so hard that the ground sank. Then the Mississippi River poured into the hole. This story is about a gray fox that hunted along the eastern edge of that lake.

Few people live on that side of Reelfoot. Steep, tree-covered hills rise up near the edge of the water, and there isn't much level ground where men can build houses or plant fields of corn.

So, all kinds of small animals make their homes east of the lake, including many foxes. But the one I am writing about was different from the others. He was a small gray fox, a kind of fox that doesn't grow very big in the first

place. So he learned to use his brain instead of his strength to survive. The other animals around Reelfoot Lake say he was the smartest fox that ever lived, and they have a story about him to prove it. It goes like this.

One winter night, as the little fox was hunting at the bottom of the steep hills, he smelled a rabbit in the cold wind. Of course, foxes hunt rabbits, and this gray fox was one of the best trackers in the woods. He followed the scent into one of man's cornfields. In a few moments, he found the animal's hiding place—a burrow of dry grass in the middle of the field.

He crept through the cornstalks very carefully. He did not want to make a noise that might frighten the rabbit away. Finally, when he was within a few feet of the rabbit's burrow, he got ready to pounce. But the instant before he leaped into the air, there was a strange sound like the flapping of wings, and something large and dark dropped from the sky. It touched the top of the rabbit's burrow then rose again and disappeared. Of course, the terrified rabbit jumped out of its burrow in a flash. It dodged this way and that through the cornfield, not knowing what had happened.

The little fox was just as startled and confused as the rabbit by the unexpected air attack, but he quickly gave chase. Since he could run very fast for short distances, he caught up with the rabbit. The gray fox was just about to grab it when he again heard the noise of the wings. Suddenly, the rabbit vanished, right in front of his eyes! Something had reached down from the sky, grabbed the animal, and carried it away into the darkness.

The gray fox stopped in his tracks. He began to search

the starlit sky. It only took a moment for him to recognize the shape of a great horned owl settling onto a limb of a large oak tree at the edge of the cornfield. In its talons hung the body of the rabbit. The owl had killed the animal the instant he snatched it from the ground.

The hair along the fox's back rose in anger. He suspected that the owl had watched him while he tracked the rabbit. Then, at the last moment, the owl swooped down from the trees, frightened the animal into the open, and caught it for himself.

The gray fox trotted to the foot of the oak tree and sat down. Above him, the owl was busy pushing the body of the rabbit into a fork of the tree limb. The fox curled his thick tail around his feet and barked at the bird.

"Say there, owl. That is nice rabbit you have."

The bird made a big show of inspecting his kill. He leaned over so far in one direction that it seemed he would surely fall from the limb, and he pretended to study the rabbit's head. Then, he leaned just as far in the other direction and looked at its tail.

"Why, yes, it is a nice rabbit, isn't it? I really hadn't noticed until now," the bird said cheerfully.

The hair on the fox's back rose higher. "If you don't mind telling me, owl, how did you happen to find that rabbit from way up in the tops of the trees? It was hidden in a burrow of dry grass. I was just a few feet from it, and I couldn't see it—only smell it."

"That is the problem with you foxes," the owl cackled down to him. "You do all of your thinking with your noses. But a smart hunter like me uses his brain. He learns the laws of nature and uses them to his advantage."

80

"And what are these 'laws of nature' that help an owl see an invisible rabbit?"

"Why the laws of the sun, the moon, the earth and sky, and all creatures of the forest. Even a dimwit like yourself must know that all things, including every owl, fox, and rabbit ever born, are ruled by these laws of nature. They are unchangeable. And if you learn how to apply them in whatever you do, there isn't a single problem in the world you can't solve—much less such a little matter as finding a hidden rabbit."

"I think I see," said the gray fox, and he casually scratched his left ear. "When I was very young and my mother was teaching me how to hunt, I noticed she had a strange habit. The instant before she pounced, the tip of her tail twitched from side to side like the rattles of an angry snake. Then, I saw that my brothers and sisters did the same thing. And they told me I also had the habit. It seems that little twitch of the tail is something gray foxes do naturally. Tell me, owl, is this one of the 'laws of nature' you study so hard?"

The owl's laughter filled the woods. "That's it! Now you are learning!" he cried. "Why, there may be some hope for you after all, fox."

"Ah, I thought so," said the fox. "Then the rabbit belongs to me. I tracked it and found its hiding place. You just watched me and stole it at the last moment."

The owl puffed his feathers out in all directions. He shook his head as though he could not believe his ears. "Stole it? Never! That would mean I had done something wrong, and how could that be? I just study the laws of nature and use them when I hunt. Is that wrong?"

81

The gray fox saw a small acorn at his feet and began to bat it along the ground. He was trying very hard to think of a way to get the rabbit back from the owl. "All I know is that no other bird of prey in these woods lets me do his hunting for him and then takes my catch."

"Well now," said the owl. "I can see you don't have much understanding of natural law. So, let me put this simply for the sake of your simple mind. If other hunters knew the laws of nature as well as I do, then maybe you would be much leaner than you are today." And once again, the owl's loud laughter filled the woods.

It was all the fox could do to control his temper. First to have his dinner stolen and then to be made fun of by the owl was almost more than he could stand. But, he knew that as long as the bird kept talking, it would not fly away with the rabbit.

"You don't sound like a bird who keeps secrets," the fox said. "Why don't you share your great knowledge of the laws of nature with me. It might improve my hunting skills. Why, I might be able to snatch game from the claws of a hawk."

"That you might!" the owl replied, and he began to strut up and down the limb, trying to look very important. The fox kept his eyes on the rabbit, hoping it might fall. But it was wedged too tightly into the fork of the tree limb.

"Of course, if I tried to tell you all that I know, we would be here for the rest of the night. And I am beginning to get hungry," the owl said. "I must keep things simple for your simple mind, fox. You should learn that summer follows spring—that bees store honey for the winter—that water runs downhill—"

Just then, the gray fox got an idea. "That's a lie!" he barked.

The great horned owl was so startled he nearly fell off the limb. He flapped his great wings and sputtered, "What? Who? Whoooo? What lie?"

"What you just said, of course," the fox replied. "I asked you a simple question. If you didn't want to answer me, you should have said so and flown away."

The owl hurried down the limb until he was directly above the fox. He puffed his feathers out in all directions and said, "Lie? I told you no lie! I gave you the simplest laws of nature."

"You did lie to me!"

"I did not!"

"You most certainly did, owl."

"*I did not, you ignorant fox!*" the owl screeched. "*When did I lie?*"

"When you said that last part—about the water," the fox answered calmly and again began batting the acorn with his paw.

"The water? Let's see—you mean that water runs downhill?"

"Yes, that's it."

For a second, the owl wasn't sure that he heard the fox correctly. He shook his head very fast (great horned owls do that when they are surprised by something), and he asked, "Do you mean to tell me, fox, that you think water can run uphill?"

"Why, of course it can. Anyone should know that. And if you don't, then you are the ignorant one, owl, not me."

"Me? Ignorant?" the owl shouted angrily. "Water can't

run uphill! That would defy the laws of nature, which is impossible."

"Which shows me how little you know of the laws of nature, owl. I thought you were just a big fake all along."

"*How little I know?*" the owl screeched. He dug his talons into the bark of the limb and flapped his wings angrily. "Any fool can tell you that water runs in only one direction—*downhill!*"

"And would you be willing to make a small wager on that, owl?"

"Of course," the owl cried. "How could I lose?"

"I say that rabbit is rightfully mine. You say it is not. I say water can run uphill. You say it cannot. If I can prove to you within the hour that water runs uphill, then you must give me the rabbit."

"If you can show me that water runs uphill, I'll catch a dozen rabbits for you!" the owl shouted down at him.

"Then follow me quickly, owl," and the gray fox ran into the woods.

He traveled fast. He ran through narrow valleys and across rocks and streams and over steep hills. The great horned owl, who carried the heavy body of the rabbit in his talons, never once got a chance to light in a tree and rest. That was part of the gray fox's plan. He knew the weight of the rabbit would make the owl very tired. And he hoped that a tired owl might also become a careless one.

Finally, the fox came to a deep valley between two hills. At the center of the valley was a small stream. He jumped this and hid in a thorny thicket. Overhead, he heard the great horned owl land in a tree. He looked through the vines and branches and grinned. The owl was tired all right, because he did not take time to tuck the rabbit safely into a crook of the tree. Instead, he just dropped it across the branch and held it with one foot.

The owl was panting from his long flight with the heavy rabbit in his claws. "Is this—huff—where I am supposed—huff, huff—to see water run uphill?"

"Yes, it is," the fox whispered. "But only if owls can be as quiet and still as a fox."

The owl hissed angrily from above him. "I'll have you know—huff, huff—that no fox alive—huff—is as quiet as an owl."

The gray fox felt like laughing. Now, it was the owl who was angry.

They waited for a long time, and the gray fox knew his hour would soon be up. He was afraid the owl would fly away. Finally, from across the little stream, he heard the noise of dry leaves crackling under the feet of an animal. The noise came closer and closer. The fox knew who was coming before he waddled into view. A groundhog named Grump.

Grump was old. He was also the biggest and strongest groundhog ever born around Reelfoot Lake. His fur was scarred from fights with hungry hunters, all of which he had won. That was why the gray fox left Grump alone. He was just too small to risk a fight with such a big groundhog. But he knew all of Grump's habits. And at this time every night, Grump came out of his den, walked down the hill, and drank from the stream.

Grump stopped at the edge of the water. He looked all around, but the owl and the fox were sitting too still for him to see them. Then, he waddled into the middle of the stream and began to drink. Every now and then, he would look up and watch and listen for enemies.

The gray fox waited until he knew Grump was nearly finished, then, as loud as he could, he shouted, "Hey, there, Grump, would you mind helping a hungry fox?"

Caught completely by surprise, Grump snorted loudly. He spun around and around in the middle of the stream throwing water in all directions. He hissed and whistled and clattered his razor-sharp cutting teeth together in a challenge. But he had no idea where the fox was hiding. So, he jumped onto the bank of the stream and began running up the hill as fast as he could, stopping every few feet to spin around and around again looking for his unseen enemy.

When Grump reached his den and hopped inside, the gray fox walked out of the thorn thicket and stared at the great horned owl.

"There you are! Did you see it?" the fox said with a broad smile.

"See what?" hissed the owl. "All I saw was you scare a stupid old groundhog."

A look of surprise came onto the fox's face. "Now, don't tell me owls are blind as well as ignorant of the laws of nature."

"*Blind?* What do you mean blind? That stream never changed direction. And the only thing running anywhere was that old groundhog."

"Well, at least you have that part right," the fox said. "Now tell me, great sharp-eyed bird, can you find the groundhog's den?"

"It is under that fallen log at the top of the hill," the owl spat down at him. "And there is a large white rock beside the opening. Does that show you how sharp my eyes are, fox?"

"Oh, yes, it does. Now, let's see if your memory is worth anything. Can you remember what the groundhog was doing before I frightened him?"

The owl began sputtering and flapping his great wings. Great horned owls have awful tempers, and although they like to make fun of others, they really hate someone's making fun of them. The gray fox knew that.

The owl screeched, "He was drinking water! What does that have to do with anything?"

"It proves my point, owl," said the gray fox with a smile. "Since the water of the stream was in old Grump's belly when he ran up the hill to his den, then water can run uphill, now can't it, owl? I have won the wager! Give me my rabbit!"

The owl's scream echoed through the woods. "*Never! Never!!* I'll never give you a thing! You tricked me!" And then, he called the fox every terrible name he could think of in owl language.

The fox kept his eyes fixed on the owl. Slowly, he brought a paw to his mouth and licked it.

"That is all right, owl," he said very calmly. "I never expected you to give me the rabbit when we made our wager. You see, I know much more about the laws of nature than you. And one of the first things I learned was that owls are not only thieves by nature, but they are also the worst possible liars."

The great horned owl raised his head toward the night

88

sky and gave a bone-chilling battle cry. Then, he dropped from the limb and flew straight at the fox with his talons gleaming in the moonlight.

"*I'll kill you, fox!*" he screamed as he fell through the air.

But an instant before the owl could sink his talons into the fox's neck, the little animal darted into the thorn thicket and disappeared. The owl was falling so fast that he almost hit the ground. He had to flap his wings hard and make a wide circle through the dense woods to again climb high into the air. By the time he could fly back to the thorny thicket, he understood the fox's plan. But he could do nothing to stop it. For as soon as he had let go of the rabbit, it slipped from the limb and dropped to the ground.

The gray fox charged from his hiding place and had the rabbit in his mouth in an instant. Without breaking stride, he tossed it across his shoulders and ran for the safety of the thicket. Once again, the owl came screaming down, but too late. His talons barely brushed the fox's furry tail as the little streak of gray jumped behind a tree and then raced into the thicket where the thorns and branches protected him.

The great horned owl flew from treetop to treetop above the thicket screeching and hissing and calling the fox awful names. The noise bothered the little fox's ears, but he knew that he was safe.

The gray fox waited in the thicket until dawn and ate the dinner that had rightfully been his in the first place. He knew sunlight hurt the owl's keen eyes, which were made for hunting at night. Finally, the bird gave a loud cry of rage and flew away.

When the fox was sure that there was no danger, he left the thicket for his own den, which was close to the lake. He stopped only once on a smooth rock in the middle of the stream. He looked at his reflection on the surface of the water. He chuckled to himself and said, "Yes, Mr. Stream, in spite of the laws of nature, you can run uphill, can't you?"

The water gurgled happily over the stones and tree roots as the little gray fox disappeared into the shadows of the surrounding forest.

"How Water Ran Uphill" and Real Life:

Some people will tell you that miracles cannot happen because they would defy the laws of nature. For instance, they say that Jesus could not have raised Lazarus from the dead (John 11:17-44) because that would have broken the laws of medicine, or He could not have turned water into wine (John 2:6-10) because that would have broken the laws of chemistry.

But the truth is that a person can only tell you how something *should* happen because of the laws of nature. He cannot say how likely it is that one of those laws will be interfered with by another force of some kind. The law of gravity tells us water should run downhill. But what if Grump drinks it and carries it uphill? That does not mean the law of gravity has been broken. It means something stronger than the pull of gravity has interfered with it.

People who argue that there are no miracles also do not believe that God is a force in man's world. To them, there are only laws of nature and nothing more. But

90

Christianity says there is God. He created the world and all the laws of nature that rule it. He is stronger than any other force that ever was or ever will be.

Christianity also says that Jesus of Nazareth was more than a man. He was the Son of God. He had the power of God and could interfere with the laws of nature. He could make something take place that could not normally take place, which is what Christians call a "miracle."

Psalm 115:3—"Our God is in heaven; he does whatever pleases him."

Genesis 18:14—"Is anything too hard for the Lord?"

Boomer

Deep in the swamps and bayous of Louisiana there are still some places where the foot of man has never made a track. It was in such a spot that a large colony of bullfrogs once lived. Their home was a deep pond surrounded by marsh and quicksand pools and tangled forests.

The colony had been there for so many years that it would be impossible to count all of the bullfrogs who were born, lived, and died in that pond. And none of them had traveled very far from their home into the surrounding swamp.

This colony had an odd custom. Every summer, when the young frogs lost their polliwog tails and were ready to become adults, all of the colony would gather in a clearing at one end of the pond. From the top of a smooth, moss-covered rock called the "Council Stone," the oldest member of the colony, the one named the Elder, leader of the other bullfrogs, would give the new adults the laws of the pond.

Year after year, his message was the same.

"Be careful when you hunt for insects near the roots of the old willow tree," he would say to them. "That is where Ashar, the black water snake, likes to hide. His stare can freeze you with terror. His fangs are deadly."

Or he would warn, "Never stay long in the tall grasses of the swamp. Norda, the heron, is a bird who hunts for frogs in such places. She may fly down upon you suddenly and claim your life."

These were just two of the rules he gave the young frogs. There were many others. But the most important warning he saved for the last moment of his speech.

"Beyond the borders of the swamp that surround our pond there lives a terrible being. He is feared by snakes and herons and all our other enemies as much as we fear them. Even before our great-great-great grandfathers were born, the elders who ruled this little colony left a warning. They told us never to leave the swamp, because it hides us from Man. And to look into his shining eye in the dark of night is certain death!"

No frog ever doubted the Elder's warning, and it kept the members of the colony deep inside the swamp. At least, no one doubted it until the year there was no rain in the swamp.

That was the worst year the bullfrogs could remember. Most of the swamp around their pond dried up. An awful fire stripped away trees and marsh grass and drove many toads, tree frogs, and other creatures that ate insects to the pond. Soon, there wasn't enough food for everyone. The bullfrogs began to go hungry. That was bad enough; but as the earth began to get hard and crack, every other kind of animal was driven to the pond because it was one of the last places that held any water. The number of creatures who ate bullfrogs doubled and then tripled. No place was safe.

On the night when the colony gathered around the Council Stone to listen to the Elder, the bullfrogs became terribly alarmed. They counted their number. Only half as many frogs were there as had gathered around the stone last summer. All of them wondered how long the drought would continue. They argued among themselves over what to do. But no one seemed to have an answer until the Elder gave his final warning to the young frogs—the warning about Man. Then, suddenly, a deep voice rang through the darkness.

"*Liar!*" it cried. Through the startled mass of green bodies pushed a huge bullfrog. He hopped into the center of the clearing in front of the Council Stone. He looked right into the Elder's eyes and again shouted, "Liar!"

All of the other frogs knew him. He was called Boomer, because his voice was so deep and so loud that in the night it could always be heard above the other sounds of the swamp. Once, Boomer had squatted at the foot of the Coucil Stone with all the other young frogs and listened to the Elder croak the laws of the pond. But after that, he lived apart from the rest of the colony. Sometimes, he would disappear for weeks at a time, and a rumor would

95

start that Norda or Ashar had eaten him.

But he always turned up again. And not once did he offer any explanation of where he had hopped off to. No one dared ask him either. The other frogs were afraid of Boomer. He was not only the biggest and strongest member of the colony, he was also one of the cleverest. He could think fast and talk faster. Boomer could make anyone who tried to argue with him look silly in front of the other bullfrogs.

It took a moment for the shock of Boomer's sudden challenge to wear off. Then, one of the frogs standing near the Council Stone cried, "You don't have any right to call the Elder a liar, Boomer."

"No right?" Boomer shouted back. "If I told you to hop into a snake's open mouth, wouldn't any frog have a right to challenge me? I have called the Elder a liar because he is a liar. And his lies have killed many bullfrogs in this colony."

"How have I lied, Boomer?" the Elder croaked from the top of the stone. "How have I hurt any bullfrog who lives in this pond?"

"You have lied by telling these frogs to stay in this tiny pond and die, when they can leave it and live. You have lied by telling them there is Man when there is no Man!"

As soon as Boomer said that, the whole colony began to croak at once. Finally, one frog gathered enough courage to inch forward and say, "Have you lost your mind, Boomer? Everyone knows there is Man."

Boomer gave a mighty hop and landed right in front of the frog. "Everyone knows there is Man," he said, making his voice sound very silly. Then, he shouted at the top of his lungs, "Have you ever seen a Man?"

The smaller frog scrambled back into the crowd in fear.

Boomer looked at the rest of the colony. "Have any of you seen a Man?"

There was no reply.

Boomer brought a webbed foot to his chin, closed one eye, and pretended to think hard. "Well, now, let's see. This Man is a real monster, or so we have been told. First of all, he stands on two legs just like old Norda, but he is a giant, bigger than any animal in the swamp. Don't you wonder how he walks anywhere. He would be so heavy that he would sink up to his neck in the mud.

"But that isn't the strangest thing about him. Man doesn't have wings or a beak or fangs to catch bullfrogs with. Oh, no, that would be too easy. Man seems to be able to take trees and turn them into whatever he needs to help him trap us. I ask you, has anyone seen an animal in this swamp take a tree and make it into anything else but a tree?"

The other frogs began croaking to one another. No one had seen that.

Boomer continued. "And he just can't have a smooth green skin like ours. He has one skin he wears all of the time. But, it can be red or brown or white or yellow. Then, over this, he wears many other skins of all different colors. These he can take off or put back on whenever he feels like it. I ask you, have you ever heard anything so silly?

"And may the sun and the moon and the stars forbid that Man should have anything quite so plain as a coat of fur. He just has to have a tuft of hair that pops right out of the top of his head!"

Boomer began to hop madly around the circle of frogs.

97

He shuffled his feet in a little dance and sang the way little frogs liked to do.

> "Man he carries a stick so long,
> And catches frogs upon its prong.
>   He has an eye that shines in the night;
> And frogs are frozen at its very sight.
>   Of eating frog legs, Man is fond.
> So, my children, never leave this pond."

The dance and the song looked and sounded so silly that most of the bullfrogs broke out laughing. But then, Boomer stopped in his tracks and spat on the ground.

"How stupid can you be?" he cried. "Of course you haven't seen a Man. There is no Man! There never was one. He is just a fairy tale—a story for little polliwogs. Yet, all of you live your lives in fear of him.

"If I told you that I turned into a bird and flew around the swamp, would you believe me? Why, of course not. But this old liar—" and Boomer shot out his long tongue at the Elder "—tells you about a monster no one has ever seen, and, whenever you hear a strange sound, you hop away in terror, hoping that Man hasn't found you. How stupid can you be?"

The bullfrogs looked at each other in confusion. No one had ever talked to them like this before. They always took for granted that Man existed.

Finally, one of the frogs at the back of the crowd said, "The reason we haven't seen Man is that he rules the world beyond the swamp. He does not come here."

But Boomer shouted, "I have been in the world beyond

our swamp three times. I never saw Man!"

All of the other bullfrogs began to croak very loudly. They were amazed by what Boomer said to them. The older members of the colony shouted for quiet. They were afraid the noise would bring their enemies down upon them.

When the other frogs stopped croaking, Boomer continued. "Would you like to know what lies beyond the swamp?"

"Yes! Yes!" they all cried.

"Only a day's march from the border of the swamp is a river. It has all the water we could ever need. Along its banks there are soft beds of grass and smooth sand. You can't count all of the stumps and logs and patches of reeds where a bullfrog can hide from his enemies.

"But the most important thing is that there is plenty of food. The moths and the dragonflies are thick as a swarm of bees!

"Here, you go hungry. Here, you are in danger night and day. This pond is much too small. But if you would make a short journey with me, you could have all of the room and all of the food you want. Why do you stay? Because you are afraid of a dream—a silly story for children—called Man."

The Elder was quiet through Boomer's loud speech. But now, he spoke up. "Listen to me, friends! It is true our life is hard in this pond. But wouldn't it be just as hard anywhere else? Remember, the snake and the heron have big families. They crawl and fly over the whole earth. Can't you remember the good years we have had in this pond, when there was enough food for everyone?"

"*Enough?*" Boomer snorted angrily. "Why should an of you be satisfied with 'enough' when you can have plenty?"

The Elder ignored him. "Here, friends, in our pond you are safer than you would be out there. Here, there is no Man!"

Boomer's voice echoed across the swamp like a clap of thunder. "Man?" he cried and jumped up on the Council Stone beside the Elder. He stared into the old frog's face and asked, "Have you with your own two eyes ever seen a Man?"

"No. But I believe he exists."

Then Boomer asked, "And tell me, old frog, do you know anyone who has seen Man? If you have, I would like to meet him or her."

"Long, long ago, the elders of this colony saw Man. They left us the rules. I believe them!" said the old frog.

Boomer spat in the Elder's face. He hopped down from the stone and again spoke to the other bullfrogs. "It is time to leave silly dreams behind you. Outside the swamp is a beautiful world. Follow me, and together we can build a new home where there is no fear."

The bullfrogs could not decide what to do. They hopped this way and that. First, they looked at Boomer, and then they looked at the Elder. They were very confused.

Finally, one of the frogs asked, "How can we be sure that you have been outside this swamp, Boomer?"

All of the other bullfrogs chimed in, "Yes! All we have is your word, Boomer. Can you prove it?"

Boomer began to grin. "So, you want proof for a

100

change? Well, at least you are beginning to show some intelligence. If you want proof, you can have it—and not empty talk like the Elder gives you. I can give you hard facts to prove there is no Man.

"I am going back to the river right now. I am going to call for Man as loud as I can—so loud that you will be able to hear me across the swamp. If Man rules that world, then let's see if he takes my life."

Instantly, Boomer jumped over the circle of frogs and headed for the swamp. A few of the younger bullfrogs followed him. But they stopped at the border of the swamp and watched him hop away into the distance.

At the pond, the meeting around the Council Stone broke up a few moments after Boomer left. A bullfrog heard a snake nearby. He warned the others, and they swam to safety.

The next day, few insects were swallowed by bullfrogs around the pond. Not a single member of the colony could think about anything but Boomer. Would he reach the river? Would Man find him? No one knew for certain. Some bullfrogs said Boomer was right; there was no Man. Others thought he was probably dead already. Really, there was only one thing the frogs could agree on. If they were able to hear Boomer's voice from the world beyond the swamp, then Man could hear him too.

When it started to get dark, the bullfrogs began to gather around the Council Stone. They came in twos and threes from many directions, whispering to each other about Boomer's bold adventure. By midnight, all of the colony were there.

Only the Elder appeared to be unconcerned. He sat on

top of the Council Stone catching insects that flew close to him. Now and then, he would stop and stare at the gathering crowd of frogs. But no one talked to him. Not a single bullfrog even wanted to look at him.

An hour passed. Then another. Whispers passed through the crowd that the Elder was right after all. Boomer had been caught by Man. But no one hopped back into the pond.

Suddenly, a young frog at the edge of the crowd shouted for everyone to be quiet. In a few seconds, the whispers stopped. Every bullfrog sat still and listened to sounds in the swamp air. Through the dozens of whistles, chirps, and growls that were the usual noises of the night, they heard a low, rhythmic hum. It was as steady as the beat of a bass drum. But it came from so far away it might have been mistaken for the soft whisper of the wind blowing through the tops of willow trees. There was no mistaking what made it—a bullfrog!

In one voice, the crowd of frogs whispered, "Boomer!"

Every eye was on the Elder. He too stopped hunting when he heard the sound. For a second, there was a worried look on his face. Then, he turned to the other bullfrogs and said, "You must believe me. There is Man."

A young frog in the crowd shouted, "The Elder has lied to us. There is no Man!"

Then, another said, "Wait! Let's not be hasty. Maybe Man has not found Boomer yet. We must be sure."

"Yes! Yes! We must wait," chanted the rest of the crowd.

So, wait they did until the night was gone and the sun began to peek above the trees. But Boomer's voice never stopped. Sometimes, when the rest of the swamp grew very quiet, the bullfrogs could understand the one word he was saying over and over again with the deepest, loudest call he had. "Man—Man—Man—Man—"

One by one, from the youngest to the oldest, they turned their backs on the Elder and the Council Stone. Bullfrog after bullfrog slipped into the dark waters of the pond and disappeared, finally convinced that there was no Man. In the end, only two remained with the Elder.

The Elder looked sadly around the clearing. He asked the two frogs who were left behind, "Why are you still here?"

They replied, "We have never seen Man. But our fathers told us about him, and they were very smart and very good frogs. We don't understand anything that has happened tonight; but we know that you have never lied to us before. Why should you lie now?"

When the Elder heard this, he slipped down from the rock and swam away.

The next night, Boomer came hopping out of the swamp into the clearing around the Council Stone. No one was there. That made Boomer a little angry. He was proud of his bold action. He expected a crowd to cheer him when he returned.

In his mouth, Boomer held a huge dragonfly. He had carried it all the way from the river. Boomer hopped onto the Council Stone and laid the dragonfly down. Then, he began to call for the other bullfrogs. They came bounding to him from all directions. Soon, the whole colony was gathered around the Council Stone.

"Now, do you believe me when I say there is no Man?"

103

he asked them. "I waited on the banks of the river and called for Man as loud as I could. But here I am. Where is Man?"

Boomer looked through the crowd. His face was full of hate. "And where is the Elder?" he croaked. "I have a gift for him."

From the dark shadows of a clump of water reeds, the old frog waddled into the moonlight. "I am here," he said.

With a flick of his long tongue, Boomer picked up the dragonfly and tossed it through the air. It landed at the feet of the Elder.

"I thought you might like some real food for a change," Boomer cried. "In one hour, I ate as many insects as anyone in this pond could catch in a whole night. And there is my proof. It is real proof—not the dreams of old frogs and little polliwogs. What more could you want?"

"Nothing more! Nothing more!" the crowd of bullfrogs shouted back to him.

"Then, follow me," Boomer said to them. "And we will go to the river and make a new home where there is no hunger and no fear of Man."

"Yes! Yes!" the rest of the bullfrogs cried. "We will follow you anywhere."

With a big smile on his face, Boomer called to the Elder, "Won't you go with us, old frog?"

The Elder shook his head slowly from side to side. "You have all of these lives to ruin, Boomer. You don't need mine."

Boomer laughed when he heard that, and the rest of the colony began laughing with him. "So, you are still dreaming about Man?" Boomer said. "Then stay here with your dreams. You will have Ashar, the black snake, and Norda, the heron, to keep you company."

With that, Boomer raised a webbed foot and shouted for the colony to follow him. He hopped down from the Council Stone and into the swamp. He was followed by a mass of happy, squirming, hopping, singing frogs. Bullfrog after bullfrog disappeared into the night. Soon, only the Elder and the two frogs who still believed him remained.

The Elder looked at the pair sadly and said, "All your friends are gone. Won't you follow them?"

The two frogs shook their heads. "This pond is our home," they said. "We like it here. Here, we are safe from Man."

The old frog climbed slowly to the top of the Council Stone. He looked across the pond. Moonlight shone on the water. Three frogs, crickets, and locusts called to one another. A gentle wind rattled the cattails in the shallow water.

"What a beautiful place this is at night," the Elder sighed. He hung his head and said, "What madness—what madness—what madness—"

The bullfrogs' journey across the swamp and through the woods, bayous, and open fields beyond took much longer than Boomer expected. When he made the trip alone, it had only taken a day. But Boomer was stronger than the others. He soon found that the very young and the very old bullfrogs could not keep up with the rest. The night after they left the swamp, they were only halfway to the river.

That wasn't the worst part. The real problem was that

the bullfrogs were confused by their new surroundings. They did not know where to hide from their enemies. So, as some grew tired and fell behind, they got lost and were easy game for snakes and birds. Every time the colony stopped for water and to rest, they counted heads. More and more frogs were missing.

Some began blaming Boomer for the deaths. Others talked about returning to the pond. But Boomer used his loud voice to encourage them and his huge size to bully those that would not listen. He kept the bullfrogs hopping forward even when they thought their strength was gone.

The deaths bothered Boomer. But he told himself that the loss of a few old or weak bullfrogs really didn't matter much. Being rid of those would make the colony stronger.

Still, Boomer was very happy late the second afternoon when he jumped through the tall grass along the edge of the river. He found a log that was partly under water. Boomer crawled onto it and called for the others. Moments later, the colony came tumbling over the river-bank and began hopping into the water. They were tired and hungry. But the river was cool, and there was a loud hum of many insects in the air. This seemed to be everything Boomer had promised.

The bullfrogs found hiding places along the riverbank. They rested and began to catch flying bugs. By the time the sun went down and the first stars could be seen in the sky, their stomachs were full and they were happy again. Bullfrog voices echoed from every direction. But the happiest voice of them all was Boomer's. He had won. Now he was the leader of the bullfrog colony, and he had led

106

his followers to a better home.

Boomer was terribly proud of himself. He was so proud that he closed his eyes and began to call as loud as he could. He wanted the Elder to hear him back in the dark, forgotten swamp.

Boomer loved the sound of his own voice, and he cried late into the night. Finally, he got hungry. He stopped calling and looked for a bug to eat. That is when he noticed something very strange. Only a few members of the colony were still calling from the riverbanks.

"Maybe they have eaten all that their stomachs can hold, and they are sleeping now," he said to himself. Just then, the biggest moth he had ever seen came flying by. He caught it with one flick of his long tongue. Boomer closed his eyes and began to call again.

It took a bright flash of light to make him open his eyes the next time. By then, there were no bullfrog voices calling along the river. Suddenly, Boomer felt frightened. Where were all of the others? And, what was the bright light that roamed this way and that along the riverbank?

The light found a bullfrog sitting in a small clump of grass just a few feet from Boomer. The bullfrog's eyes glowed like tiny stars. Now Boomer could see the light came from something large and dark floating near the riverbank. At first, he thought it was a big log. But then, he saw that it moved against the river current. It drifted nearer to the bullfrog in the grass. Boomer called to him. He told him to hop away. But for some reason, the bullfrog would not move. Suddenly, there was a quick motion, and the other bullfrog was gone.

Boomer started to jump into the water and escape. But

he said to himself, "Why should I be afraid of something just because I don't understand it?"

Then, the bright light swept along his log without warning. It found him! Boomer wanted to hop away, but he found that he could not move his legs. All he could do was stare into the very middle of the light, which was drawing closer and closer to him. He wondered what it could be. He tried to remember anything he had seen in his life that was like it.

But there was nothing in Boomer's world even similar to an electric lantern. That was a tool of Man. And Man was so different from a bullfrog that Boomer could not have imagined anything like him.

He had no idea that Men built boats from trees. He didn't know that they sometimes took their boats and a lantern and a long stick with sharp metal prongs on one end and rowed along the riverbanks looking for bullfrogs. He didn't know, until it was too late, that the bright light of the electric lantern would cause a bullfrog to sit still long enough for Men to row their boat close to him and spear him.

Boomer heard strange noises drifting over the water. But he did not believe in Man. So, how could he know the sound of a human voice?

"Hey, Jack, look at the size of this bullfrog," one man in the boat whispered to the other. "I told you I heard a big one down here a couple of nights ago."

Boomer had so many questions. But he had asked them too late. Boomer's life ended suddenly on the sharp points of Man's frog-gig.

Far away in the middle of the swamp, the Elder and his

two friends sat quietly near the Council Stone. They had listened for hours to Boomer's constant hum in the distance. Then, as suddenly as it began, the voice was gone, never to be heard again.

The Elder lowered his eyes and stared sadly at the still water of the pond.

"Man," he said, and then hopped slowly into the shadows of the water reeds and disappeared.

"Boomer" and Real Life:

Many years ago, there lived a man who did not want other people to believe in God. He would stand in front of a big crowd and shout, "If there is a God, I challenge Him. Let God strike me dead where I stand." Then, he would wait for a moment or two and say, "You see, I am still alive. There is no God!"

That caused some people to doubt that there was a God. But remember Boomer? He went to the river and called for Man. When Man didn't come that very night, Boomer said there was no Man. But that never changed the fact that Man did rule the world beyond the swamp.

Man was so different from a bullfrog that even though some of the elders had seen him in the past they had a difficult time describing him. God is so powerful, so different from us—how *can* we describe Him? The answer is that we have to describe God in ways that we understand even though the words we use for Him are very poor. Still, they are the only words we have.

In the Bible, Abraham, Moses, King David, Paul, John, Peter, and many others wrote about God and the wonderful things God has done. They described Him with the very best words they had. Men may choose to ignore their words and say there is no God. But, like Boomer, those men will also come to a "river" one day. It is the "river" called "Death." There, whether they chose to believe in Him or not, they will meet God.

Psalm 14:1 — "The fool says in his heart, 'There is no God.'"

The King of the Fish

Mountain lions once ruled the High Sierras of California. These big tawny cats, also called cougars, roamed from mountaintop to mountaintop hunting for food and guarding the borders of their lands. They were the kings of the Sierra Mountains.

One spring, near the top of a tall peak, a baby cougar was born. For many weeks, his mother did not allow him to leave the small cave where they made their home. The mountainside was steep, and there were many dangers in the nearby forest for a cub who did not yet know how to defend himself. But, later in the summer, his muscles and bones grew stronger. Also, his fur changed color. He lost the soft, spotted coat of a youngster, and his hair became light brown and stiff. And even though he was very clumsy, never taking many steps without tripping over his own

113

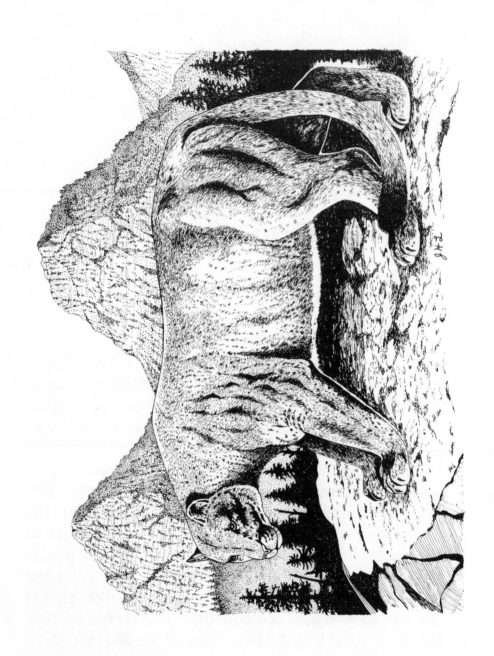

huge paws, he was big enough to follow his mother on short hunting trips.

On these hunts, the mother cougar tried to teach her cub how to stalk deer and rabbits. He learned a few hunting secrets by watching her. But most of his time was spent chasing butterflies or wrestling with his mother's long tail. So, whenever the two of them really needed food, she left her young son at the cave and went into the mountain forest alone to hunt. Each time she left, she warned him to stay very near their home and if ever he found himself in danger to call for her as loudly as he could. She would come running to save him.

The cub did his best to obey her; but he had no brothers or sisters with whom to play. There was nothing to do all day long at the cave but sleep. Soon, he grew lonely and bored. He began to wander farther and farther into the forest near his home. In the forest, there was adventure and new things for him to see and do.

He discovered the giant sequoia trees, which were so tall that to see their tops he had to crane his neck upward until he fell onto his back. At the bottoms of these huge trees, he often found red pine squirrels hopping here and there in search of food. When he chased them, the little animals would climb up and up and up to the very tops of the sequoias. Then, they would scold him and drop seed cones down at him. He would laugh and shout, "I am prince of the mountain. One day I shall be your king!"

He saw colorful birds and wild flowers and many kinds of strange animals in the Sierra forest. Once, he had to learn the hard way why young cougars were not allowed to play with baby skunks. It took a week for the awful smell of their spray to come out of his fur.

But the most exciting discovery the cub made on his journeys was a mountain pool. He found it late one afternoon not too far from his cave. The pool was wide and shallow and clear. It was fed by a rushing stream that poured down from the top of the mountain. In that pool were many rainbow trout.

Now, the cub had never seen fish before, and to him they seemed very strange and wonderful creatures. Their scales were as colorful as the feathers of a mountain bird. They never came onto the land like every other animal he knew in the forest. Now and then, one of them would leap into the air and catch a flying insect in its mouth. And, whenever he reached beneath the water and tried to touch one, it darted away from his paw faster than anything he had ever seen in his life.

Just as soon as the young cougar's mother returned home from the hunt that day, he led her to the pool. He showed her the trout that lived in it. He made her tell him everything she knew about fish: how they breathed under water and swam quickly with mighty strokes of their broad tails and caught bugs for food.

By late summer, this pool had become the cub's favorite place to play. Mountain lions are not as afraid of water as many other kinds of cats. So, the young cub learned to swim there. At first, he did it just to chase the fish. Then, he found that on a hot summer day the cool water felt good.

At the center of this pool stood a pair of large white boulders. Between them was lodged the trunk of a tree. It had washed down the mountain early that spring when

melting snow and heavy rains turned the stream that fed the shallow pool into a raging river. The log had a thick limb that stretched over the surface of the water. The cougar cub liked to swim to those boulders, climb the tree, and sit on the limb. He pretended that it was a throne and he was the king of the mountain. The trout swimming underneath him were his loyal subjects.

One hot afternoon while his mother was away hunting, the cub wandered down to the pool. But instead of swimming to the log where he usually played, he stretched out upon a flat rock by the water's edge to watch his friends, the fish. The sun was warm on his fur. The air was still, and there was a sweet smell of honeysuckle in his nose. The trout swam lazily this way and that in search of food. The little cub began to feel very sleepy. Finally, he thought he would close his eyes just for a moment. And that is how the young cougar fell asleep.

That might not sound like a bad thing for him to do. But it was a terrible mistake. Time and time again the cub's mother had warned him never to sleep in the forest away from the safety of their cave. She knew that in the wilderness there were many dangers for her cub. He needed to always be alert for the sight, sound, or smell of an enemy. But it happened to him so unexpectedly.

It is very likely this would have been the last nap the young cougar ever took if it had not been for one of the trout. The fish spied a dragonfly buzzing over the water right in front of the cub. It leaped into the air, caught the insect in its mouth, and landed on the surface of the pool with a loud flop. Water splashed into the young cougar's face, and he was awake in a flash.

118

Some feeling deep inside the cub's heart warned him that he was in danger. Suddenly, he heard the rustle of grass behind him. The sound was so soft that a human ear probably would not have detected it. But mountain lions have a very keen sense of hearing. At first, he thought of running for the safety of the cave. But he knew that he was too slow and clumsy. A strong hunter would have caught him before he got ten feet. Instead, he followed the instincts nature had given to him at birth.

When mountain lions are in danger, they climb trees. The closest tree to the young cougar was the one in the middle of the pool. So, he sprang high into the air and landed in the pool with a great flop. Behind him, something leaped from the tall grass. He heard the loud clack of fangs snapping shut on empty air. He had escaped not a second too soon.

The cub swam as hard as he could for the boulders. Then, he scrambled up the tree trunk to the safety of the limb. He turned. There, standing on the rock where he had been sleeping only seconds before, was a big coyote. Its gray fur was soaked. The cub had splashed water all over the animal when he jumped into the pool.

The young cougar was terribly frightened. He knew that he was no match for the strong jaws and great speed of a full-grown coyote. But he realized that he was safe for the moment. First of all, coyotes do not like to swim. And even if the gray hunter could have reached the boulders in the middle of the mountain pool without swimming, he could not climb the tree.

The coyote shook himself very hard and then began to prowl silently around the rocky edge of the mountain pool. Hungrily, he watched the little cub. He was very angry. He had not expected the young cougar to awaken when he did and leap into the pool where he could not follow.

The cub gathered his courage and growled, "You're going to be sorry for that!"

The coyote stopped in his tracks and tried to look very surprised. He smiled slyly at the cub and asked, "Sorry for what, Your Majesty?"

"For trying to sneak up behind me and catch me!" the cub snapped back at him.

The coyote just chuckled and said, "But you are wrong, young cougar. I would never think of hurting you. Why you are a prince of the forest. I just came to this pool on a little business. If I had known you were sleeping here, I would have checked it another day."

"Checked it for what?" the cub asked.

The coyote sat down. He was a very cunning hunter. He thought that if he acted like the cub's friend he might be able to lure him from the safety of the tree. He answered, "Every spring the ice and snow on the mountaintop melts and water fills this pool. Also every spring, the fish swim upstream from the valley below and stop here. But by late summer the stream feeding this pool from the mountaintop dries up. And when that happens, the fish are trapped. Day after day, the pool gets shallower. And finally, when the water is low enough, I come and catch the fish and eat them. They are really very tasty. Why don't you come down here and join me, young prince? I can teach you how to hunt them."

But instead of falling into the coyote's trap, the young

cougar grew even more angry. He raised his head into the air and cried for help as loudly as he could. Then he stared angrily at the coyote and said, "In a few moments, it won't be fish that are caught here, but you!"

From a distant ridge echoed a terrible war cry. His mother had heard his voice and was coming to his rescue. The coyote instantly came to his feet, and the hair on his back and shoulders stood on end.

The young cougar dug his claws into the bark of the tree. His little eyes flashed. He said, "You are a liar, coyote. You tried to kill me, but you failed. I won't forget that. So, you had better listen to me and remember what I have to say to you! I may only be a cub today, but soon, I am going to grow into a mighty king. And when I am king, I'll chase you away from this mountain and see to it that you never return!"

The coyote tucked his gray tail between his legs and disappeared into the tall grass. He wanted to be miles from that pool when the mother cougar arrived. If she found him there, she would certainly kill him.

From his perch high above the pool, the cub watched the coyote running over a distant ridge of rocks. He began to think about the animal's story. He stared at the stream that fed the mountain pool. As the coyote had said, it was no more than a tiny trickle. However, a wide stream of water still poured down the mountainside from the pool. If that did not change, it would soon be dry and the fish would be food for the coyote.

The more the cub thought about this, the worse he felt. He liked the fish. They were his friends. And one of them had even saved his life. He did not want them to be eaten by the terrible coyote. But he would not be strong enough to chase the coyote from the mountain for many, many months. And he could now see that the mountain pool would dry up in just a few weeks.

I must save them, the cub said to himself.

Down the tree he climbed. He crouched upon one of the white boulders with his nose just above the water. As soon as one of the trout swam by he squalled, "Swim downstream! This pool is no longer safe." But the fish just darted away from him in fear.

Another trout came near him. "Escape while there is still time!" cried the young cougar. But this fish also fled from the sound of his voice.

The cub became very upset. He again climbed to his perch on the limb so he could see all of the fish in the pool. Then, as loudly as he could, he shouted at them. "What is the matter with all of you? Can't you see that I'm trying to help you? If you don't leave this pool soon, you will be trapped. The coyote will come back and eat you."

But none of the fish seemed to pay any attention to him. They just kept swimming calmly around the pool looking for insects to eat.

That made the young cougar angry. "I am a prince of the mountains," he said. "One day I'll be your king. You must obey me. I want all of you to swim downstream this minute!" But they would not.

Down the tree he scampered once more. He said to himself, *If the fish won't listen to me, I'll just have to make them leave the pool.* He leaped into the water. He splashed this way and that. He tried very hard to herd the fish towards the stream that poured down the mountain-

122

side to the valley. But the fish were terrified of him. Whenever he came near them, they darted in every direction except the one he wanted them to go. After ten minutes of swimming and leaping and splashing, the young cougar saw that he had not made a single trout leave the pool.

Suddenly, his mother burst from the woods surrounding the mountain pool. She was wild with fear for the life of her son. The scent of the coyote was still strong around the pool. She saw her son standing in the shallower part of the pool soaked with water and very tired.

"Are you all right?" she asked with alarm. "What has happened?" And the cub told her the story of how the coyote tried to catch him and how the fish saved his life. He also showed her that the pool would soon dry up leaving the fish as helpless prey for the coyote.

The young cougar trotted out of the pool and shook himself all over. Then, he said to his mother, "Why don't the fish listen to me? I only want to help them. Besides, I am a prince, and one day I'll be their king!"

His mother licked him on the head lovingly and answered, "Even though you will one day be the king of this mountain, you will never be the king of the fish. To them, you are a terrifying creature. They live in water while you live in air. The sight of your paws and the sound of your voice in their world is strange and frightening to them. No, my son. The only way that you could ever become king of the fish is if you could turn into a fish. Then they would understand your voice and follow you to safety."

The mother cougar nudged her son with her nose. "Now, we must go home; and until you are strong enough to fight the coyote, you must not return to this pool."

The cub walked sadly towards his cave. He knew this would be the last time he would ever again see his friends, the fish.

"The King of the Fish" and Real Life:

Some people say they cannot accept Christianity as the truth because Christians believe that God actually became a man in the person of Jesus of Nazareth. They cannot understand why God would need to take the form of a human being.

Of course, there are many reasons why that had to happen. But one of the simplest can be learned from the story of the young cougar and the fish. The cub wanted to help the fish escape the danger that they were in. But he was so big and strange and frightening to them that they fled from him.

The Bible tells us that God is so different from man and has such great power that no man could look directly at Him and live.

God has always wanted to help men escape the danger they face from Satan and sin. What better way could God have done that than by coming to earth in the form of a man? As a man, He could speak to people face-to-face and tell them of His deep love. He could show them the way of escape. The young cougar was not able to turn himself into a fish in order the help the fish. But God has the power to do anything. So He performed a great miracle. One night, in the little town of Bethlehem, Jesus was born. And He was both man and God.

Men who once obeyed God just because they were afraid of His power loved Jesus and obeyed His teachings. The words God spoke in those days through Jesus Christ were recorded in the gospels of Matthew, Mark, Luke, and John. After nearly two thousand years, God's words still lead men to safety.

Of all the miracles recorded in the Bible, this was the greatest. God became man, and for a little while He walked among us.

John 1:1, 14—"In the beginning was the Word, and the Word was with God, and the Word was God. . . . The Word became [man] and lived for a while among us. We have seen His glory, the glory of the one and only Son, who came from the Father, full of grace and truth."